THE CHINESE

HOW THEY LIVE AND WORK

Volumes in the series:

The Chinese

HOW THEY LIVE AND WORK

T. R. Tregear

PRAEGER PUBLISHERS
New York · Washington

BOOKS THAT MATTER

Published in the United States of America in 1973
by Praeger Publishers, Inc.
111 Fourth Avenue, New York, N.Y. 10003

Library of Congress Cataloging in Publication Data

Tregear, Thomas R
THE CHINESE
(How they live and work)

SUMMARY: A cultural overview of China
examining the effect of the revolution of
1949, Mao Tse-Tung, and present government structures on the way of life in city
and country.

1. China—Description and travel—
1949– Juvenile literature. [1. China—
Social life and customs] I. Title.
DS711.T677 1973 915.1'03'5 72–93301

Printed in Great Britain

Contents

List of Illustrations

(*All the photographs are reproduced by kind permission of the Society for Anglo-Chinese Understanding, London*)

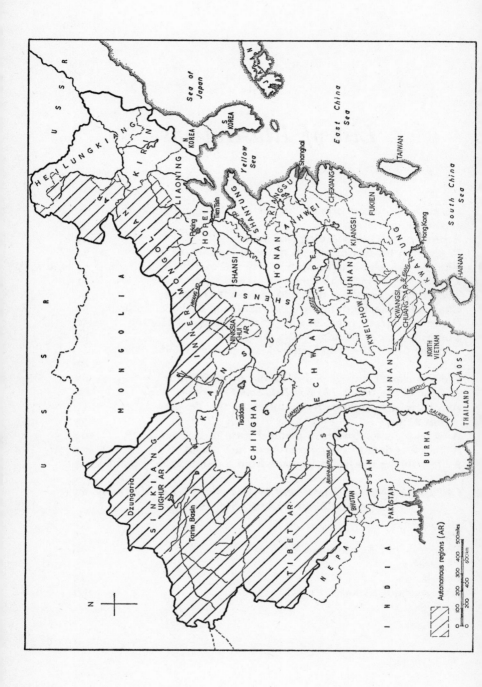

Introduction

THIS is a short book on a big and exciting subject. Because it is short it is often necessary to deal in generalisations, which, while being broadly correct, will be subject to innumerable exceptions. A case in point is the general pattern of the commune, the variations of which are infinite.

It has been found convenient to use the term Liberation, *Kai-fang*, constantly to signify the takeover of power by the Communists from the Nationalists in 1949. Some westerners may reject it as a misnomer but in China it has universal usage and for very large numbers it did mark liberation from oppression.

It will be noted throughout the book that comparisons drawn are of China before and after Liberation rather than between China and the Western world. This, in the author's view, is by far the more profitable approach, shedding light on the reasons for policies and actions, on the granting or restricting of certain freedoms and on the priority given to this or that activity.

We are viewing a country engaged on conducting a gigantic experiment, the significance of which the rest of the world has not yet fully comprehended. It is ultimately nothing short of attempting to change man's nature from that of self-seeking to unselfishness. Its methods may be challenged; its objective is unassailable. It is endeavouring to replace personal profit as the incentive to man's work and activities by one of service for the whole people. Should it prove successful, the results would be world-shaking. The static philosophies of the past 2,000 years have been suddenly replaced by dynamic Marxism. It remains

9

to be seen whether China's age-long capacity for absorbing invaders will once again dominate and produce its own unique interpretation.

Readers may be disappointed by the paucity of statistics. One of the casualties of the Great Leap Forward of 1958 was the break-down of the State Statistical Bureau, which had been carefully and steadily built up after 1949 into a reliable and professional department. It compiled *Ten Great Years: Statistics of the Economic and Cultural Achievements of the People's Republic of China* in 1960. Since then no systematic or firm figures have been published.

Chinese place-names are always a problem partly because different systems of romanisation are used in various atlases but, more importantly, because during the last thirty to forty years the names of towns and cities have been changed—more than once in some instances. Throughout this book the *Times Atlas* place-names have been used. The term 'North-East' is now used for what was formerly Manchuria.

Lack of space has precluded any discussion of life as lived under Chiang Kai-shek and the Kuomintang in that other part of China, Taiwan.

ABBREVIATIONS

AR	Autonomous Region
CCP	Chinese Communist Party
FYP	Five-Year Plan
GPCR	Great Proletarian Cultural Revolution
KMT	Kuomintang (Nationalists)
NPC	National People's Congress
PLA	People's Liberation Army

I

The Country and the People

THE People's Republic of China has an area of 3,657,765 square miles. A figure of this size, for most people, is meaningless and it is therefore more helpful to attempt a comparison with, say, Europe or North America. Superimposed on Europe, China would extend from one end of the Mediterranean to the other. Its most northerly point in the North-East (Manchuria), latitude 54°N, would cover Moscow and the island of Hainan, latitude 18°N, would be in the region of Khartoum. Superimposed on North America it would stretch from Vancouver Island to Cape Breton Island and from James Bay in Hudson Bay in the north to Jamaica in the south. This vast area includes the following regions: China Proper 1,532,800 square miles; Inner Mongolia 747,366 square miles; Sinkiang 550,579 square miles; Tibet 463,320 square miles; the North-East 363,700 square miles. With these figures we can compare the area of the USSR, 8,597,000 square miles; of Canada, 3,842,144 square miles; and of the USA, 3,022,387 square miles.

China's land frontiers are very extensive and touch no less than eleven countries: Korea, USSR, Outer Mongolia, Kashmir, India, Nepal, Bhutan, Burma, Laos and North Vietnam. The most extensive and important is that between USSR and China. There are several disputed frontiers, notably in Kashmir, North-East India and along the Ussuri River in the extreme north-east, north of Vladivostok. The disputed area between Burma and China has been peacefully settled. China also has a long seaboard, smooth and shallow north of Shanghai, highly indented, with many fine natural harbours, south of that city. The continental shelf below the Yellow Sea and South China Sea, probably rich in oil, is a potential source of international tension.

This great land stands, roughly speaking, at three main levels. (a) Tibet is a huge tableland, having a general level of 16,000ft or over, out of which mountain ranges of 5,000 to 10,000ft rise. It is bounded by the Kunlun and Altyn Tagh in the north and the Karakoram and Himalayas in the south. This is a vast, desolate land of wide, wind-swept valleys, almost uninhabited, save for two regions. In the extreme south-east where the Tsangpo (Brahmaputra) flows from west to east before cutting through the Himalayas into Assam, lie the three towns of Lhasa, Shigatse and Gyantse, the heart of the Lama religion and an area of considerable development in recent years. In the extreme north-east, lying at a lower level (6,000–9,000ft) than the main plateau, is the Tsaidam basin, which is largely salt desert and semi-desert steppeland. Tibet is a vast area of inland drainage.

(b) At a lower level of between 2,000 to 6,000ft and to the north of Tibet lie the two great plateaux of Sinkiang and Inner Mongolia. Sinkiang contains within its borders two large basins of inland drainage, the Tarim and Dzungaria. The Tarim basin is bounded by mighty mountain ranges, the Kunlun to the south, Pamirs to the west and Tien Shan to the north. All the rivers, including the Tarim itself, flowing from these mountains lose their waters in the sands of the Taklamakan, one of the world's most desolate deserts. Ringing this desert and based on the river is a chain of oases, which formed the line of the historical Great Silk Road. The remarkable Turfan basin (940ft below sea level) lies to the east of the Tarim basin and south of the desert and semi-desert plains of Dzungaria, where the oilfield of Karamai is located. The vast steppelands of Inner Mongolia stretch away east and north-east to form the southern and eastern edges of the Gobi desert of Outer Mongolia.

Physical

(c) To the south and east of these great highlands lies China Proper, the name given to the eighteen provinces of old Imperial China (Hopei, Honan, Shantung, Kansu, Shensi, Shansi, Chekiang, Kiangsu, Anhwei, Kiangsi, Hupeh, Hunan, Szechwan, Fukien, Kweichow, Yunnan, Kwangtung and Kwangsi). This is the region of the great river basins of China in which 95 per cent of the population lives. Across it from west to east flow four great rivers—the Hwang-ho (Yellow River), Huai-ho, Yangtze Kiang and Si Kiang. In the north the Hwang-ho rises deep in the highlands of north-east Tibet and descends on to the plateau of Inner Mongolia, where it winds in a great northward bend round the Ordos desert and through the loess lands of Shensi. It turns east through the Tungkwan gorges to issue at Sanmen on to the North China Plain, a great alluvial geosyncline of the river's own making. As the Hwang-ho flows through the soft, fine loess it picks up an enormous load of silt during the summer spate. When it enters the Tungkwan gorges it carries 34 kilograms per cubic metre (2·26lb per cubic ft) of silt—over thirty times as heavy a load as the Nile in spate carries. As the river enters the plain the flow is checked; it can therefore no longer carry its load, which is spread over the land, resulting in flooding. During nearly three millennia the Chinese have attempted to combat this menace by building dykes to contain the river. As more and more silt was deposited between the lines of dykes so the bed of the river rose, and with its rise the dykes had to be built higher and yet higher until the bed of the Hwang-ho today lies well above the surrounding country-side. Thus, in times of spate, if the dykes break, the resulting floods are the more disastrous because when the river level falls the flood waters cannot return to the main stream. For many centuries the river has been known as 'China's Sorrow'. The river has changed its course fundamentally many times, finding an outlet to the sea now north of the Shantung peninsula and now south, joining the waters of the Huai-ho. From 1851 until 1938 the Hwang-ho flowed north into the Po Hai but in 1938 the dykes were deliberately broken by orders of the Nationalist government, flooding 20,000 square miles in an effort to stem the advancing Japanese army, resulting in the loss of nearly a million lives—an action which did not endear the government. In 1946 it was restored to its former course by international action.

In 1955 the People's Government published *The Multi-purpose Plan for permanently controlling the Yellow River and exploiting its water resources* and immediately started to implement it. A large dam has been built at Liuchia in Kansu to control the torrent waters and a key dam at Sanmen where the river issues on to the North China Plain. This dam, 90 metres high, retains a lake which now stretches back nearly to Sian on the Wei-ho. Supporting this main dam 47 others have been built or are being built across the main river and its tributaries. Their chief purpose is the retention of silt and the control of flow but they also serve to improve irrigation and navigation and to generate HE power. Just before the completion of the Sanmen dam in 1960 friction between China and USSR led to the sudden withdrawal of the latter's advisers, technicians and plans resulting in serious delay in the completion of the hydro-electrical part of the scheme.

South of the Hwang-ho is the Huai-ho, which finds its outlet into the Hwang Hai (Yellow Sea). The watershed between the two systems is barely discernible and the Huai plain enjoys the same unenviable reputation for flooding as the Hwang-ho. It was chosen by Mao Tse-tung in 1949 as the first big scheme for water conservation. The order went out 'emphatically correct the Huai'. Ten dams of considerable size have been built on the river and its tributaries. The largest, 230ft high and 1,700ft long, is at Futzeling on the Po-ho. These dams, together with vast dyking, have prevented serious flooding since their construction and have improved irrigation. A new canal, the Peh Kiangsu Canal, has been cut from the Hungtze Lake to the sea, improving both drainage and navigation.

Greatest of China's river systems is the Yangtze Kiang. It is 3,494 miles long and has a catchment basin more than twice that of the Hwang-ho. (Cf Mississippi 2,348 miles; Thames 210 miles.) Its source is high up in the Tibetan plateau. Thence it flows in deep, narrow gorges from north to south for about 1,000 miles. It then turns east and flows through the Red Basin of Szechwan, a great lake of Cretaceous time, now filled with deep deposits of red sandstone. It cuts its way through the Tapa Shan in the famous awe-inspiring Yangtze Gorges, which are 100 miles long, to emerge on to the low lake-studded basin of Hupeh, Hunan and Kiangsi. Here it receives three great tributaries, the Han Kiang on the left bank and the Siang Kiang, emptying into the Tung Ting Hu, and the Kan Kiang, into the Poyang Hu, on the right. The Yangtze at Wuhan, 600 miles from the sea, in the heart of this basin is nearly a mile wide and has a difference between winter and summer levels of 45ft. The volume of water passing Wuhan is enormous. In summer in normal years it is over 1 million cubic ft per second; in 1931 when there was serious flooding, the flow was 2·8 million cubic ft per second. The average summer velocity at this point is nearly 6 knots and the river is therefore able to carry most of its heavy load of silt through the narrows as it cuts its way through the Tapieh Shan between Kiukiang and Anking on to the delta plain and so to Nanking and Shanghai.

Last of China's great river systems is the Si Kiang (West River), which drains the southern provinces of Kwangtung and Kwangsi (Chuang Autonomous Region). Rising in the Yunnan and Kweichow plateau, it flows from west to east finding its outlet to the South China Sea in a large delta south of Canton. Its main stream flows between Hong Kong and Macau. It is smaller than either the Hwang-ho or the Yangtze and lies almost entirely within the tropics.

China has within its borders almost all types of climate (with the exception of those associated with the western coast of continents, ie Mediterranean, Temperate Oceanic and Equatorial). They extend from the high cold desert of Tibet through the hot desert of Sinkiang and the continental steppelands of Inner Mongolia to the temperate and subtropical monsoon lands of China Proper. The controlling factor influencing the whole country is the alternation of pressure from intense high over the Asian heartland in winter to a corresponding low in summer, resulting in outflowing cold dry winds in winter and onshore warm moist air in summer. Rainfall decreases steadily from an annual total of 85in in Hong Kong in the south-east to a mere 4in in Kashgar in the north-west. The 15in isohyet, which runs from north-east to south-west, has divided the country throughout the centuries into pastoralist in the north-west and arable farmer in the south-east. It is interesting to note that the Great Wall, built by Ch'in Si Hwang Ti (221–207 BC), follows this isohyet very closely. Unhappily, greater variability and uncertainty are associated with the sparser rainfall of the north, which is thus subject to severe drought and consequent famine. The south-eastern coastal regions from Shanghai to Hainan are subject to occasional destructive typhoons from July to September. It is not surprising that so great a land mass as China produces a wide range of temperatures. Harbin, in the far north, has a mean monthly average temperature of −5°F (−21°C) in January while Canton is experiencing 56°F (13°C). The land heats up quickly in spring and summer, resulting in high temperatures everywhere. The diurnal range of temperature in the dry interior is great. 'Fur coat in the morning, fine silk at midday' is the order of the day in winter.

In the drier northern half of China Proper the soils are predominantly pedocals, ie limey and calcareous. In the far west desert soils are extensive. Shensi and Shansi are covered with loessial soils, in places to a depth of 250ft. There are also extensive areas of saline soils, particularly along the banks of the lower Hwang-ho and along the littoral of Kiangsu and Hopei. A good deal of the soil in the Yangtze basin is neutral purple and brown forest soil, especially in the Red Basin of Szechwan. As one goes farther south into regions of heavier rainfall where the land is subject to greater leaching, the soils become increasingly acidic (pedalfers) and in Kwangtung and Kwangsi they have marked lateritic tendencies.

The natural vegetation reflects the climate and the soil. Steppe and semi-desert grass characterise much of the north-west lower land with coniferous forest in the mountainous areas.

B

There is an increasing amount of deciduous forest farther south, which in its turn gives place to broad-leafed evergreens, camphor and bamboo and finally to tropical vegetation in Kwangtung, Kwangsi and Hainan. In the plains and river basins in China Proper, which have been densely settled and intensively cultivated, little of the original cover remains. Soil erosion to a serious extent has resulted. Since 1949 strenuous efforts at afforestation to combat this evil have been made.

CHINESE ORIGINS

The first traces of primitive man in China were discovered in 1927 in a cave at Chou K'ou Tien near Peking. 'Peking Man' or *Sinanthropus Pekinensis* lived here some 500,000 years ago; his skull is said by experts to show marked Mongoloid characteristics. There is no further evidence of man in north China and Mongolia until Palaeolithic times, about 50,000 years ago, when elephant, rhinoceros and stag were hunted. A long period follows in which no further traces of human habitation have yet been found.

Then, in 1922, a Swedish archaeologist, J. G. Andersson, made extensive finds at Yang Shao, near Loyang, of a well-established neolithic culture flourishing about 4,000 to 5,000 years ago. The finds included polished stone tools, axes and adzes and pottery decorated with fine flowing designs in black and red, which have given the name Painted Pottery to this culture. These and further finds in Kansu revealed a settled people, based on a primitive slash and burn agriculture and hunting. In 1928 evidence of another neolithic culture was unearthed in the north-east at Lung Shan, Cheng Tzu Yai near Tsinan. This is distinguished from the Yang Shao by its pottery, which is hard, black and burnished and is known as Black Pottery culture; it is subsequent to the Yang Shao. In addition to more advanced farming techniques, it reveals permanent settlements of walled villages, burials indicating class differentiation and the practice of scapulimancy, ie consultation of the oracles by means of bones. These two neolithic peoples occupied sparsely the north of China some 6,000 years ago.

In 1934–5 further archaeological discoveries brought to light the existence, about 2,000 years later, of a highly organised society and advanced civilisation living in the region of the confluence of the Hwang-ho and Wei-ho. These people, the Shang, are undeniably Chinese. They lived in substantial houses in mature towns, were governed by a king and had an advanced differentiation of classes. Beautiful and highly developed cast bronze vessels served their elaborate ritual. The bones used in their scapulimancy were incised by markings which are the earliest form of Chinese writing. By means of these inscriptions, Tung Tso-ping, oracle bone authority, believes that the Shang king P'an Keng moved his capital to Mo, near Anyang in 1384 BC.

Were these Shang people the indigenous successors to the Painted Pottery and Black Pottery people or were they immigrants from the earlier civilisations of the Near East? Scholars are still not agreed on the answer. Those favouring the second contention argue that the Shang civilisation, with its sophisticated society, its highly developed metallurgy and its advanced agriculture, could not, in so short a time, have developed *in situ* and must have been imported from the west. These arguments have now lost much of their force. Recent discoveries, particularly those of pre-Shang bronzes at Chengchow, point fairly conclusively to the continuity of culture from Yang Shao and Lung Shan to Shang and there is now a strong consensus of opinion that the Chinese are indeed indigenous and that this region is the cradle of their civilisation.

POPULATION

China's first attempt at a scientific census was made in 1953. It was made on a *de jure* basis, that is, on persons habitually present rather than on the more usual basis of *de facto*, persons actually present. The result was startling as it revealed over

100 million more people than any of the estimates of this century. The total for Mainland China, including national minorities, was 582,603,417. Of this figure 506,738,390 resided in the eighteen provinces of China Proper, 41,732,529 in the North-East (Manchuria), 11,666,397 in the three municipalities of Shanghai, Peking and Tientsin, leaving only 22,466,101 inhabitants in the whole of the vast territories of Inner Mongolia, Jehol, Sinkiang, Sikang, Chinghai, Tibet and Chamdo. Since 1953 there has been considerable movement of Chinese into Sinkiang and into the North-East, especially into the province of Heilungkiang, partly for reasons of industrial and agricultural development and partly for political reasons.

Census figures revealed that nearly 87 per cent of the population of China Proper was rural. Demarcation between rural and urban is not precise. Generally places of 2,000 or less were classified as rural, but, if engaged in mining or industrial activity, they were recorded as urban even though less than 2,000. Men outnumbered women by 107 to 100. This proportion is changing in favour of women due to a number of factors, the chief of which are the rise in the status of women and the removal of the spectre of famine, when female infanticide was common.

Another arresting feature of the 1953 census figures was the age composition; 41·1 per cent of the population was under 18 years of age and 86·5 per cent less than 50 years. Compared with Europe and even with USA this reveals a very youthful people. Since 1949 preventive medicine and public hygiene have been pursued, resulting in a big fall in the death rate and an increase in the expectancy of life from 27 years in 1900 to 54 in 1958. There are, therefore, more old people living today than formerly but the youthful proportion is still maintained due to the phenomenal fall in the infant mortality rate.

No firm figures of population have been published since 1953. The most reliable estimates put the present figure at about 750 million, which means a growth of about 7 million a year. Comparable figures for other countries are India 573 million,

Population

USSR 241 million, USA 207 million and UK 55 million. The People's Government has regarded this growth with changing degrees of optimism and caution, varying to some extent with the demands of production and the state of harvests. In early days after liberation unlimited growth was welcomed. More recently family planning has been strongly advocated. There are clinics in every town of any size. Families of two or at most three are considered ideal, a notion which finds acceptance in the towns now that mortality rates are low but one which makes slower progress in the rural areas. Advice on contraceptives is readily available. Sterilisation and abortion can be performed on a doctor's recommendation. Late marriages are urged, for men 25–7 years and for women 21–3. China is well on the way to defeating Reverend Thomas Malthus's three population checks of war, pestilence and famine and is resorting to his solution of late marriages.

The racial composition of the country is diverse. About 94 per cent of the people are Chinese, who themselves are differentiated into Han Jen (Jen = man) and T'ang Jen. The Han Jen are roughly those north of the Tsinling Shan axis and are taller, sharper featured and more phlegmatic than the T'ang Jen, who are darker, broader featured and more volatile. The T'ang Jen claim to be of purer Chinese stock than the Han Jen, who have been subject to so many invasions from the north.

The remaining 6 per cent number about 35 million and contain China's national minorities, the chief of which are the Chuang people of west Kwangsi, the Uighurs (Turki) of Sinkiang, the Moslems (Hui) of Kansu and Chinghai, the Tibetans and the Mongolians. The Manchus, remnant of the Ch'ing dynasty, are now widely scattered and fully integrated. Large aboriginal tribes (Yi, Miao, Lolo, Yao, T'u chia) are located in the mountains of the south-west.

LANGUAGE

Language is one of the great forces for the development of a race.

(*Sun Yat Sen in 'San Min Chu Ih'*)

In a country so vast it is not surprising to find that even within the bounds of China Proper there are many dialects so different from each other as to constitute different spoken languages. The average citizens of Peking, Canton, Shanghai, Foochow and Chungking, when they meet, find conversation very difficult, if not impossible, and the average countryman from these districts would not make the attempt. In recent years strenuous efforts, notably through radio, are being made to overcome this handicap and to cultivate a common dialect—*p'u t'ung hua*—that all can understand. Throughout Chinese history, however, there has been a saving factor in this communication difficulty, which is that the written language is common to them all. This fact has played a very large part in maintaining the unity of the Chinese people throughout the centuries.

Chinese writing has developed from the crude pictographs found on oracle bones of the Shang dynasty (1730–1122 BC). These pictographs or characters became stylised and increased in number until today there are over 23,000. Since the Chinese have no alphabet, characters have to be learned by rote. Happily, knowledge of some 4,000 to 5,000 is adequate for normal purposes. Nevertheless, learning even this number is a severe tax on memory and time. Many attempts have been made in the last 100 years to romanise the language, with only limited success. The difficulty is that many characters, entirely different when written, have the same sound. For example, Mathews's *Chinese-English Dictionary*, which contains only 7,785 characters, has no less than 92 with the sound of *fu*. The problem is further complicated by the fact that Chinese vowels have at least four different tones, which significantly alter the meaning of the word. The latest attempt at romanisation uses over 60 phonetic symbols. It would seem that, until a sufficiently unified spoken language is achieved, no really satisfactory romanisation is possible. In the meantime the People's Government is tackling the problem at the other end by simplifying about 1,000 of the old characters. While this will mean that more people will be literate and that children in school will spend less time learning their characters, it will also mean that much of the former literature, written in the old characters, will be less comprehensible.

The Tibetans, the Mongols and the Uighurs each have their own language and literature unrelated to Chinese. The many tribes or minority peoples each have their own spoken language. At the end of last century and the beginning of this, Christian missionaries attempted to create a written script for one or two of the tribes, notably that by Samuel Pollard for the Miao people. Since Liberation much more work has been done in this field and most, if not all, tribes now have their own scripts based on the Latin alphabet.

HISTORICAL LANDMARKS

We have seen how a mature civilised people under the Shang rulers emerged from the neolithic Yang Shao and Lung Shan cultures. Not long after the Shang capital had been moved to a site near Anyang, strong virile tribes, probably of Turki stock, under Wu Wang, invaded from the west, overcame the Shang and founded the Chou dynasty (1122–255 BC), the longest dynasty in Chinese history. The land, which had been apportioned under the 'well' system during the Shang period, was parcelled out among relations and allies, titles such as duke, earl and baron were conferred and a feudal system ensued, lasting with ever-decreasing efficiency to the end of the dynasty. Wu Wang died in 1116 BC. The Duke of Chou held an exemplary regency for the young successor for seven years.

The Chou dynasty is most noteworthy for its vast literature and the development of philosophical thought. *Tao Te Ching*, a number of poems or chapters, contains the core of the teachings of Lao Tzu, the father of Taoism, a deep philosophy of quietism and naturalism. Confucius (552–479 BC), who was probably 50 years younger than Lao Tzu, was the founder of a philosophy of right behaviour of the princely man, taking for his model the Duke of Chou mentioned above. Neither Lao Tzu nor Confucius themselves wrote anything, but the *Confucian Analects* and the works of Mencius (372–289 BC), Confucius's famous disciple, contain the teachings which became the official philosophy and the text-book of government of China for more than 2,000 years.

During the last 250 years of the Chou dynasty the feudal system broke down and a period known as the Warring States ensued. The small, vigorous, semi-barbarous state of Ch'in in the north-west developed a centralised military system, which was destined to make one of the greatest changes in Chinese history. Ch'in advanced eastward, conquered all the quarrelling feudal states and brought them all together, establishing in 255 BC the first unified state of China with Ch'in Shih Hwang Ti as its first emperor.

Ch'in Shih, by stern dictatorial methods, abolished feudalism and the communal cultivation of the land, instituting private ownership and a system of taxation. By harsh forced labour he built the Great Wall as protection against the threatening nomads of the north and west. He unified writing and standardised the coinage and weights and measures. In an endeavour to blot out all memory and influence of the former period of Chou he ordered all historical and classical books to be burnt, exempting only those of a practical nature or dealing with divination. During his short rule the borders of China were extended southward to the sea in Kwangtung. The Ch'in dynasty fell in 206 BC, four years after his death, leaving an indelible mark on China's future and also an unsavoury reputation. The famous Han historian, Ssu-ma Ch'ien wrote:

Ch'in has the same customs as a tiger or wolf. It is avaricious, perverse, eager for profit and without sincerity. It knows nothing about etiquette, proper relationships and virtuous conduct and, if there be an opportunity for material gain, it will disregard its relatives as if they were animals.

Ch'in was succeeded by the long Han dynasty, which lasted from 202 BC to AD 220. The centralised system of government was retained and strengthened but its basis was changed. Every effort was made to recover the ancient books and Confucianism was adopted as the official philosophy. It has had its periods of decline but remained the standard of behaviour until the twentieth century, penetrating so deeply into the culture of the people that successive invaders have been absorbed into it. During Han times there was great territorial expansion. The Great Wall was extended westward to Tunkuang (the Jade Gate) and Turkestan (present Sinkiang) came under Chinese rule. The strong nomadic tribe of Hsiung-nu (Huns) was so harassed by Han armies that they were forced to migrate westward. It is interesting to speculate on the degree of Han responsibility for the Hun overthrow of Rome. The conquering of Turkestan led to the establishment of the famous Silk Route and Imperial Road, lines of trade between China and Rome. Han emperors also expanded southward, conquering Tonking and North Annam and establishing a sea route to India. The fall of this great dynasty is the oft-repeated tale of decadence, of court extravagance and intrigue, of internecine war and of peasant oppression and revolt.

There followed a period known as the Six Dynasties when the country was divided, with barbarian kingdoms in the north while the south maintained Chinese traditions. It was during this time of disillusionment and disappointment that Buddhism, offering a gospel of hope and escape, made its first impact on China. Monks from India entering via the Tarim Basin and the Jade Gate so impressed the barbarians of the Six Dynasties, especially the King of Wei, that they adopted Buddhism. Later it was accepted by the south and Emperor Wu Ti of the Liang dynasty (502–56) became an ardent convert. Fa Hsien (399–414) was the most famous of the many Chinese Buddhist monks who made long journeys to India for more study and to bring back sacred writings.

Unity was restored by the short-lived Sui dynasty (589–618), during which there was great canal building, notably the New Pien canal which ran from the Yangtze via the Huai-ho to Kaifeng, and thence by the Hwang-ho to the capital at Chang-an (Sian). This canal was necessary because the economic heart of the country was shifting from the lower basin of the Hwang-ho to that of the Yangtze. Canals were essential for the transport of tribute grain to the court at the northern capital.

Sui was succeeded by the T'ang dynasty (618–906). Under Emperor T'ai Tsung it became great in all senses of the term. It achieved political stability, systematising the examination system, the only means of entry into the civil service. Big estates were reduced in size and there was some equalisation of land holding which increased prosperity. Great expansion of territory took place. Turkestan and Korea again came under Chinese rule. Chang-an the capital vied with Baghdad as a great international meeting place. But the bubbling life and vitality of T'ang is most clearly revealed in its cultural maturity, in its graceful Buddhist statuary, its lively figurines, its beautiful green and white ceramics, its landscape paintings, but above all its poetry. Once again Court extravagance, growing power of governor-generals and oppression of the peasantry led to downfall.

Then followed a period of disunity when nomad invaders established kingdoms (Liao and Chin) in the north while Chinese culture and tradition were maintained first by the Northern Sung (960–1127) and then by Southern Sung (1127–1279) in the south, until both north and south were overwhelmed by a Mongol invasion. Temuchin, having united various Mongol tribes, was proclaimed 'The Mightiest Khan, Genghis Khan'. He proceeded south in 1215 and defeated the Kitans (Chin dynasty) in north China. Between 1219 and 1224 he conquered Turkestan, Persia and Syria, and he died as he renewed his invasion of China. This was completed by Kublai Khan, who founded the Yuan dynasty (1280–1368). He estab-

lished his capital at Cambaluc (the present site of Peking), remains of which are the Bell and Drum Towers, which each
housed a garrison of 1,000 guards. This was a military regime
with an army of both men and horses trained under iron discipline to great endurance. It developed a very efficient post-
horse rapid communication system extending to Turkestan.
Kublai Khan built a great fleet and attempted the invasion of
Japan, but the fleet was utterly destroyed by great storms. The
Japanese view this deliverance in the same light as the English
regard the defeat of the Spanish armada.

In spite of the fact that Kublai Khan drew all sorts of men,
Syrians, Turks, Arabs and Venetians into his service, civil
government was incompetent for it excluded Chinese from
high office in its administration. The dynasty is remarkable in
that the first real Western contacts were then made and the
first real extensive knowledge of China obtained by Western
people. Friar John, Carpini and William of Rubruck, delegates
from the Pope between 1245 and 1253, brought back reports
which differed markedly from those of Marco Polo (1271–95).
The Grand Canal from Hangchow to Peking was built in this
period. The Mongols, being pastoralists, never really comprehended the settled agricultural way of life. Their armies became
decadent, their administration oppressive and slothful. The
Chinese under Chu Yuan-chang drove them back to their
steppelands, where they quickly recovered their vitality.

Chu Yuan-chang became the first emperor of the Ming
dynasty (1364–1644). Great efforts were made to restore native
Chinese culture and traditions. Bridges, highways, tombs were
restored. The Grand Canal, which had been neglected, was
rehabilitated and the Great Wall repaired. Chu attempted to
carry out social and land reforms but was frustrated by the
wealthy landowners. This was a period of cultural grandeur. In
literature the Chinese classical novel, with romantic historical
themes, achieved great heights and drama flourished. Ching-te
Chen in Kiangsi, renowned for its white kaolin, became the
pottery metropolis of China and remains so to this day. It was
here that the famous Ming blue and white porcelain was pro-

duced. The first sea approaches by Europeans were made in this dynasty. The Portuguese arrived in 1517, the Dutch in 1622 and the British in 1637. Yet once again Court extravagance and decadence led to internal unrest and left the last of the Mings easy prey to northern invaders.

Manchu tribes, under Nurhachu, descended from the northeast and founded the Ch'ing, the ultimate imperial dynasty (1644–1911). Ch'ing must receive closer study than we have been able to give to earlier dynasties. Two of China's greatest emperors, K'ang Hsi (1661–1722) and Ch'ien Lung (1736–96), ruled each for the Chinese cycle of 60 years during the first 150 years, during which Chinese civilisation was held in high esteem in the West. Under K'ang Hsi, who ascended the throne when he was seven and took over the reins of government at fifteen, China's frontiers were again extended and the area under her control was greater than under any previous dynasty except the Yuan. The Mongols were subdued in 1697 and Tibet was brought under Chinese suzerainty in 1780, since when it has always been regarded by the Chinese as an integral part of their empire. At the same time the Russians were extending their territory far east into Siberia, north of the Amur River. This led to tension and finally to the signing of the Treaty of Nerchinsk in 1689, the first treaty concluded by China with a foreign power.

A wide field of internal development was undertaken; the currency was reformed, corruption dealt with and the waterways and canals yet once again repaired. K'ang Hsi welcomed Jesuit missionaries, notably Ricci (1601), to his court, not for their Christian doctrines but for their mathematical science, as he was at pains to point out to them. The Jesuits at this time achieved a considerable integration of Christian doctrine and Confucianism, which was repudiated by Rome.

Ch'ien Lung, equally as industrious, able and energetic as K'ang Hsi, was also a scholar. He further extended China's frontiers to include the Tarim basin and Nepal and received tribute from Indo-China and Burma. Both reigns are outstanding for their achievements in the arts, particularly in ceramics but also in painting, lacquer work and carving. Most famous of Chinese novels, *The Dream of the Red Chamber* was written at this time.

Near the end of Ch'ien Lung's reign Britain made her first determined effort to open trade officially with China. In 1793 Lord Macartney went as George III's ambassador to the imperial court. Profound ignorance of each other's customs and etiquette together with China's sense of superiority and self-sufficiency ('. . . nor do we have the slightest need of your country's manufactures') made the visit fruitless, as also was a similar attempt by Lord Amherst and a Russian envoy in 1816. The only foreign trade officially permitted was at Canton through the Chinese Guild of Merchants, known as the Co Hong. This was restrictive in the extreme and a continual frustration to the thrusting Western merchants, led by the British.

Matters came to a head in 1839 when China prohibited the lucrative trade in opium, and seized and burnt large stocks of opium held in foreign 'factories' or warehouses in Canton. War with Britain resulted, in which China with its antiquated arms was defeated. The Treaty of Nanking in 1842 opened five ports (Canton, Shanghai, Ningpo, Foochow and Amoy) to foreign trade. Other nations, notably USA, France and Belgium, were quick to avail themselves of this. The island of Hong Kong was ceded to Britain. Extra-territoriality, that is, the right of foreigners in China to be tried by their own courts, was established. Christian missions were allowed to enter and propagate their religion. Thus began a century of military, economic and cultural invasion by the West. Bitterness on both sides led to a second war with Britain between 1856–60 and again China was beaten. The resultant treaty opened a further ten ports, including the Yangtze ports, to trade. Foreign ships could sail right up the river to Hankow. Each port had its concessions, areas of land held by foreign nations in which their own rule of law ran. Embassies were opened in Peking and further concessions were made to missions and foreign travellers. Kowloon was ceded to Britain. Russia took the opportunity of occupying all land north of the Amur River and east of the Ussuri River, while France occupied Indo-China.

While the next 35 years saw no further large inroads by foreigners into China's sovereignty, it was a period of great internal disorder in the form of peasant risings against the Manchus, including the T'ai P'ing Rebellion (1850–64) and five serious Mohammedan risings in Kansu, Shensi, Yunnan and Turkestan. The T'ai P'ing alone is estimated to have caused some 20 million deaths and great devastation. Underlying this unrest is the population explosion of the two previous centuries of peace and prosperity. The estimated population in 1662 was 100 million and in 1850 414 million. Unfortunately, there was no corresponding increase in cultivable land. The inevitable result was a great land hunger, speculation, an increase in absentee landlordism and oppression of the peasant farmer, who became tenant or landless—a situation which continued until 1949 and was largely responsible for the downfall not only of the Ch'ing dynasty in 1911 but also of the Kuomintang in 1949.

Foreign imperialism (*Ti kuo chu ih*) resumed its pressures when a europeanised Japan started on its attempt to achieve its dream of a Greater Japanese Empire. Japan and China quarrelled over supremacy in Korea, war broke out in 1894, China was signally defeated and, by treaty, Japan obtained Formosa (Taiwan), the Liaotung peninsula and an indemnity. This was the signal for the powers to make further gains in their various spheres of interest—France in Annam and mining concessions in Yunnan; Russia by lease of Dairen and Port Arthur and control of the Chinese Eastern Railway in Manchuria; Great Britain by the lease of the New Territories and a strong financial position in the Peking-Hankow Railway. USA contented itself with the economic opportunities which these concessions gave her under 'most favoured nation treatment'.

Under these humiliations the Ch'ing dynasty was fast disintegrating. Some effort to avert final downfall was made by the liberal reform group at Court with Emperor Hsuan Hsu's backing but this was cut short by the Dowager Empress Tz'u

Hsi (Old Buddah). Cruel, energetic, reactionary, she seized and imprisoned the emperor and, in 1897, diverted a peasant rising, the Boxers, into anti-foreign channels. The embassies in Peking were besieged and atrocities against foreigners were widespread. Again foreign armies were landed and Peking taken. The Court fled and humiliating peace conditions were imposed, including an indemnity of $303 million.

Meanwhile, under the leadership of Dr Sun Yat Sen, liberal elements at home and abroad were developing, albeit disjointedly, a revolutionary movement which aimed at the overthrow of the Manchus and the establishment of a modern, democratic republic. After an abortive rising in 1895, Sun had to flee and henceforth organised revolutionary societies mainly from Japan. Some sporadic attempts at reform were made by the tottering government and in 1909 provincial assemblies were convened, but the Court opposed the demand for a national parliament.

The secret revolutionary party planned simultaneous uprisings for December 1911 but the accidental explosion of a bomb in the revolutionary headquarters in the Russian concession in Hankow in October 1911 sparked off the revolution prematurely. However, the revolt spread quickly. Belated

---

Headquarters of the Huapei Brigade of the Li and Miao Autonomous Chou (Region) in tropical Hainan Island. The early rice crop is being brought in for threshing (note the three threshing machines), weighing and packaging. Part goes to the State in taxation and part to the various production teams.

A production team at work weeding rice fields in Ningsia Hui Autonomous Region. Here the alkaline land has been reclaimed and irrigated, producing good harvests. Note the corn crop and the wind-break in the background.

promises of reforms were rejected by the revolutionaries, who declared China a republic and elected Sun Yat Sen its first president. Yuan Shih-kai, Commander-in-Chief of the Imperial army in the north, playing his cards skilfully, arranged the peaceful abdication and retirement of Emperor Hsuan T'ung (P'u Ih) and came to terms with the south. So the Manchu dynasty died and the Republic of China was born in 1911.

For the sake of peace between north and south Sun Yat Sen relinquished the presidency in favour of Yuan Shih-kai, who commanded the army. Yuan, who had ambitions of himself becoming the emperor of a new dynasty, was assassinated in 1915 and chaos ensued. The government of the country fell into the hands of various military governors, notably Wu Pei Fu in the centre, Chang Tso Ling in the north and the Christian general, Feng Yu-hsiang in the north-west. From 1915 to 1927 is known as the 'War Lord' period, one of lawlessness, corruption and oppression of the peasantry.

Sun Yat Sen, the recognised leader by all liberal elements, made his headquarters in Canton. Here he formed his Nationalist (Kuomintang) party and proceeded to build an army with Chiang Kai-shek as Commander-in-Chief. Disillusioned by the failure of the Western powers to support his efforts or to

---

Production teams working on the terraced loess wheat lands of Shensi. The elaborate terracing is essential to prevent soil erosion but makes mechanisation difficult.

Designed and built in China, the *Hong-chi* (Red Flag) combine harvester is the standard machine now in use on the extensive state farms and large communes of the North China plain and the North-East. In the rice lands only 7hp and 10hp hand tractors can be used.

protect China against Japanese post-war rapacity, he turned for help to Russia and Communism. Here, too, he produced his famous *San Min Chu Ih*—the Three Principles of the People, Nationalism, Democracy and the People's Livelihood—which had a profound influence especially in its promise of 'Land to the Tiller'. In 1925 he died. The Chinese Communist Party (CCP) was formed in 1921 and co-operated with the KMT (Kuomintang) in Canton in building an army, which undertook the Northern Expedition in 1926. Advancing north through Hunan with promises of land reform, it overran Wu Pei Fu's demoralised forces and took Wuhan. Chiang moved down the Yangtze valley to take Nanking, which he established as the Nationalist capital.

Almost immediately the KMT and CCP fell out and there followed a bitter struggle for supremacy which was not resolved until 1949. The Communists, whose military strength was small, retired to the uplands of central China. Around Chingkangshan in south-east Honan they established soviets and there defied Chiang's repeated and bloody efforts to dislodge them until, in the summer of 1934, with an army of 900,000 and vast preparation, he broke their resistance. Then followed the epic Long March. A Red army of 90,000 began a 6,000 mile trek, fighting its way westward to the borders of Tibet, thence northward, finally arriving 20,000 strong at Yenan, Shensi. It was during the hardships of this march that Mao Tse-tung was acknowledged undisputed leader and the close bonds of comradeship forged, which were to hold for thirty years.

Meanwhile external aggression in the form of Japanese imperialism was again rearing up. Manchuria was annexed and the state of Manchukuo established, the Japanese placing ex-emperor Hsuan T'ung (P'u Ih) as its puppet head. Nanking was powerless and the League of Nations merely protested. Chang Hsueh-liang, son of the former war-lord Chang Cho-ling, and his army were driven south on to the North China plain by the Japanese. Hitherto fairly loyal to Chiang Kai-shek but now exasperated by his obsession of wiping out the Communists rather than facing the Japanese menace, Chang's mutinous officers seized Chiang Kai-shek during a visit to Sian in 1935. Ironically his life was saved largely by the intervention of Chou En-lai in an endeavour to promote a united KMT-CCP front against Japan. In 1937 Japan invaded China. The Nationalists offered little resistance. Government was removed from Nanking to Chungking in the natural stronghold of Szechwan. Although there was nominal co-operation between Nationalists and Communists against a common enemy, the only real resistance came from the latter, centred in Yenan. Much the same guerilla tactics as were used in central China by the Communists against the KMT were used successfully against the Japanese. So it was that when the war ended in 1945, the CCP had gained a wide reputation as the true upholders of the nation's sovereignty.

With an end to the war the two parties rushed to seize the liberated territory. The Nationalists, with USA aid, occupied the greater part of China Proper. The bitter civil war was renewed in a country that had known no real peace since the turn of the century. The next three years were a period of chaos, incompetence and corruption occasioned largely by galloping inflation. During the Sino-Japanese war (1937–45) price levels had risen from an index of 100 to 156,195. In spite of attempted reforms, by July 1948 the figure had risen still further to 287,000,000. In August 1948 a currency reform edict ordered the issue of 2 gold yuan paper notes in exchange for one silver Mexican dollar, the only viable currency. This edict was disobeyed literally at risk of execution. By May 1949 the exchange rate had moved from 2 to 6,000,000. Wages and salaries had to be turned immediately into goods or they were quickly valueless. Banks offered 25 per cent on deposits of three weeks. Government servants were forced to indulge in corruption if they were to live. To this demoralisation must be added the political oppression meted out against any liberalism amongst students and workers and also the forced labour directed to building defence works against the Red Army as it moved southward. This Red Army was preceded by propaganda almost identical with that of the Northern Expedition in 1926 promising land reform to the peasants. Whereas in 1926–7 these promises were never redeemed, the Communists had already carried through land reform in the areas they controlled in the north and therefore were given credence. Nationalist forces, equipped expensively with USA weapons, retreated and disintegrated and Chiang Kai-shek with the remnants of his army embarked from Canton to take possession of Taiwan. The victorious Communists proclaimed the People's Republic of China and the event is referred to universally in China as *Kai fang* or Liberation.

2

Mao Tse-tung: His Thought and Writings

'GUIDED by the thoughts of Chairman Mao and the CCP . . .' or words like them preface virtually every report or article of politician, cadre, farmer, engineer, doctor, teacher and athlete on work they have done, or are setting out to do, in China since the beginning of the Cultural Revolution in 1966. The study of Mao's works is declared to be, and widely believed to be, essential to right thought and right action. In recent years hundreds of millions of copies of the Little Red Book *Quotations from Chairman Mao Tse-tung* have been printed and distributed throughout the land. Clearly, if one is to have any sort of realistic picture of present-day China, one must have at least a rudimentary idea of what nearly a quarter of the world's people is, day in and day out, exhorted to study and act upon. To do this effectively it is essential to have some picture of Mao's background.

Mao Tse-tung was born in 1893 in Shaoshan, Hunan, in the heart of the Yangtze valley, at a time when the Manchu dynasty was tottering to its final fall in 1911. From birth until he came into power in 1949, Mao knew only a country rent by external wars, civil wars, the terror of war-lords and bandits, the indignities of foreign direction and exploitation, a country with no firm central government, shot through with corruption and, above all, a peasantry oppressed by all and sundry. Such an environment has made an indelible impression on Mao's thought. From it springs his faith in, and compassion for, the

39

poor peasant, his bitter hatred of their oppressors and of foreign
imperialism and his belief that force alone could achieve the
unity of his country and its equality with other powers.

His father was a 'middle' peasant, hard and grasping, for
whom he had no affection. He ran away from home and became an impecunious student. By reading, study and association
with others he progressed through the liberalism of J. S. Mill,
Adam Smith and Jeremy Bentham and then, by meagre
Marxist pamphlets, to communism at a time when it was
dangerous to have even liberal leanings. It is significant to
remember that Mao's brothers, his sister and his wife were all
killed or executed in pursuance of their politics and that Mao
himself came within an ace of sharing the same fate.

One of his earliest interests was in physical fitness. His first
publication was on this subject in *New Youth* in 1917. Through
the years he retained this keenness: witness his annual swims
across the Yangtze—no mean feat when the river is in spate.
Robert Payne, writing of him in 1946, said:

> *Then Mao came into the room . . . He looked like a surprisingly
> young student . . . There was about him a kind of quietness such as
> you find among people who have lived much alone . . . He was fifty-
> three and looked twenty.*

Between 1921 and 1923 he was engaged largely in organising
urban labour unions in Hunan, but in 1924, with the alliance
between the young Chinese Communist Party (of which he
was a founder member) and Sun Yat Sen's Nationalist Party,
he began organising the peasant movement in south China.
This was an important change; from now on Mao placed
reliance on the peasantry rather than the urban worker as the
basis of revolution, one of the main differences between
Chinese and Russian communism. In 1927 he wrote his *Report
of an Investigation into the Peasant Movement in Hunan*, which had
a very cold reception from his colleagues. The CCP at this time
was very doctrinaire and was following directives from Moscow.
Although Mao was a founder member of the Party, it was not
until after the fierce and bitter struggle with Chiang Kai-shek

and the KMT, culminating in defeat and the epic retreat of the Long March, that he became the undisputed leader of the CCP and that his thought and writings began to receive full attention and carry authority.

After the Long March, which welded the remnant into a dedicated group, the CCP established itself in the dry loess lands of Shensi and made its headquarters at Yenen. It was here that Mao did his main writing and teaching and here that he tried out his theories in practice among the poverty-stricken peasants of this famine-bedevilled region.

In spite of his deep distrust of dogma, Mao emerges as a strict Marxist-Leninist, holding firmly to dialectical materialism as opposed to the metaphysical. The latter, he has maintained, relies on external forces and is static in its approach. He has equated it with the Confucian saying, 'Heaven changes not and the Way too, changes not', ie that man is conditioned by forces external to himself. On the other hand, dialectical materialism is dynamic, inside forces being the important element of change. Within everything in the universe there are contending forces, which, by their interaction, lead constantly to change and development. External elements are of only secondary importance. These contending forces, known as contradictions, give rise to the most important fundamental law of dialectical materialism, the law of unity of opposites. Probably the most important of all Mao's writings is on this subject and is called *On Contradiction* (August 1937).

This struggle between contending forces Mao has held as the very essence of life. The absence of struggle is synonymous with death. Antagonism is essential. Writing in the midst of the Sino-Japanese struggle, when confronted with a military foe, he says, 'It is a good thing, not a bad thing, to be opposed by an enemy.' Thus confronted, one is able to see clearly what has to be done. This ideal of struggle, of contradiction, is carried through class struggle against imperialist, capitalist and landlord, into every aspect of economic and domestic life, into the field where the farmer contends with nature, into the factory where the worker strives with problems of inadequate tools or new means of production into the school, into the hospital, home and playing field.

> *There is infinite joy in struggling against Heaven; there is infinite joy in struggling against Earth and there is infinite joy in struggling against man.*
> *Happiness is struggle.*

Mao Tse-tung, writing recently on this subject, says:

> *For countless years, in the minds of people in general, happiness savours of enjoying a leisurely and peaceful life, while struggle has signified tension, fatigue and hardship. Happiness and struggle have appeared to be two diametrically opposite things.*

But Mao demands of the people continuous struggle, continuous revolution. Much of the Cultural Revolution upsurge stemmed from a fear on the part of Mao and his colleagues that the present generation, lacking memory's spur of former oppression and want, would become fat and contented and so lose the will to struggle, which would spell disaster. Therefore there must be periodic campaigns which would enable the people to see the enemy, quicken class consciousness and so maintain the revolutionary spirit.

Mao has had a deep distrust of dogma and bookishness. As early as 1930 he wrote a pamphlet entitled *Combat Bookism* in which he states that 'without investigation there is no right to speak'. Later in *On Practice* (July 1937) he develops this theme.

> *Man's knowledge depends mainly on his activity in material production, through which he comes gradually to understand the phenomena, the properties and laws of nature, and the relations between himself and nature; and through his activity in production he also gradually comes to understand, in varying degrees, certain relations that exist between man and man. None of this knowledge can be acquired apart from activity in production ... Man's social practice is not confined to activity in production, but takes many other forms—class struggle, political life, scientific and artistic pursuits; in short, as a social being, man participates in all spheres*

of the practical life of society. Thus man, in varying degrees, comes to know the different relations between man and man, not only through his material life but also through his political and cultural life (both of which are intimately bound up with material life).

Thus, he says, experiment and experience lead to thought (theoretical knowledge), which must then be tested in practice before it becomes correct knowledge and which, in its turn, leads to fresh thought and so on. Mao expressed this later in *Where do Man's Correct Ideas Come From?* (May 1963) in these words:

It is often necessary to repeat many times the process of going from matter to spirit and spirit back to matter, ie from practice to knowledge and from knowledge back to practice, before correct knowledge can be achieved. This is the Marxist theory of knowledge, that is, the dialectical materialistic theory of knowledge.

This belief that knowledge depends essentially on material practice is the main reason why there is a constant pressure on all theoreticians, be they administrators, researchers, managers, teachers and the like, to spend some of their time each year working with their hands in the field or on the factory floor.

All personnel of our State agencies, writers, artists, teachers and scientific research personnel, should contact the workers and the peasants by making use of all possible opportunities. Some go to factories and the countryside to take a look. This is called 'looking over the flowers from the back of a galloping horse' but it is better than not looking at all. Others may stay in the factories or rural villages for a few months and there make investigations. That is called 'getting down from the horse and taking a look at the flowers'.

Much of his writing clearly shows his urgency for increasing the confidence of the masses, the need for initiative and experiment both in thought and action and the need for courage to make mistakes. In his famous 'Let a Hundred Flowers Bloom' speech (March 1957) he urged just this on intellectuals.

> *Blooming means giving rein to everyone in speech so that people*
> *may dare to speak, criticise and argue . . . To convince people, one*
> *can only persuade them instead of coercing them. The result of*
> *coercion is always negative. It will not do to try to subdue people by*
> *force. It may be done with an enemy but can never be done with a*
> *comrade or friend.*

This particular experiment misfired badly. There was a
spate of criticism of the regime, much of it unbridled, which
ended in suppression and subsequent long-lived loss of confidence amongst the intelligentsia—a very negative result.

From the time when Mao Tse-tung began to work among
the rural communities in 1927, he unswervingly and passion-
ately placed his faith and reliance on the poorer peasant
masses. There is an ancient Chinese saying, 'The people are the
water and the ruler the boat. The water can support the boat
but it can also sink it' (Hsun Tze, 300 BC). Mao's modern
Communist equivalent is, 'We are the fish and the people are
the water of life to us. We do not ride over the people but swim
with them.' This has been a guiding principle with him. His
appeal has been consistently to the poor peasant, for whom he
has had a deep compassion. Moreover, only in so doing can he
move towards the classless society on which he has set his eyes.
Howard Boorman says of him:

> *Mao Tse-tung has stood out as one of the very few national*
> *leaders in twentieth-century China who has shown sustained con-*
> *cern with the hardships, brutality and grinding want which charac-*
> *terised the lot of the poorer peasants. This concern required no*
> *sophisticated Marxist rationale.*

Mao's attitude to women has had a profound effect on the
country and on the course of the revolution. In securing for
them equal status with men he has expected them to tackle the
same physical and mental work as men and to shoulder the
same responsibilities. His expectation has met with amazing
response; women are working alongside men in farm, factory,
engineering and administration.

Perhaps, more than anything else, Mao's undisputed leadership has derived from his single mindedness and his unswerving faith in ultimate victory throughout all adversity. Right or wrong—and he has made many mistakes—he regards all tasks and all enemies as conquerable.

We despise all enemies strategically and take account of all enemies tactically. And earlier: *All reactionaries are paper tigers. In appearance reactionaries are terrifying but in reality they are not so powerful. From a long term point of view it is the people who are powerful.*

His aim, the creation of a strong, modern, industrialised Communist China, which involves nothing less than the conversion of 700 million people from an individualistic way of thought to one in which the good of the whole people predominates, has been pursued with a ruthlessness which belies his outward quiet, urbane appearance. Right at the beginning of his political career he wrote in his *Report of an Investigation into the Peasant Movement in Hunan*:

A revolution is not the same as inviting people to dinner, or writing an essay, or painting a picture, or doing fancy needlework; it cannot be anything so refined, so calm and gentle or so mild, kind, courteous, restrained and magnanimous. (Confucian virtues.) *A revolution is an act of violence whereby one class overthrows another.*

Much of his life, at least up to 1949, was engaged in fighting and the brutalities of war; much of his thought and writing is devoted to military theory and tactics. Yet Mao, like so many of China's former rulers, has been a poet. Whilst much of the subject matter of his poems is concerned with the revolution and the political scene, his verses reveal a contemplative side, full of warmth, friendship and love of beauty; they are also full of classical allusion. The following lines were written when he returned home to Shaoshan after an absence of thirty-two years. They have been translated by Jerome Ch'en and

Michael Bullock and are taken from Dr Ch'en's *Mao and the Chinese Revolution.*

> *I curse the time that has flowed past*
> *Since the dimly remembered dream of my departure*
> *From home, thirty-two years ago.*
> *With red pennons, the peasants lifted their lances;*
> *In the black hands, the rulers held up their whips.*
> *Lofty emotions were expressed in self-sacrifice:*
> *So the sun and moon were asked to give a new face to heaven.*
> *In delight I watch a thousand waves of growing rice and beans,*
> *And heroes everywhere going home in the smoky sunset.*

In 1962 Mao Tse-tung's writings were collected and published in four volumes under the title *Selected Works.* During the Great Proletarian Cultural Revolution (GPCR), excerpts, parables and texts were gathered from these works and published as *Quotations from Chairman Mao Tse-tung.* This 'Little Red Book', of which tens of millions of copies have been sold, has had a profound influence on both the thought and action of the mass of Chinese people.

3

How the Country is Run

UNTIL the revolution of 1911 when the Chinese Republic was formed and a constitution drawn up, China and Great Britain were the only countries in the world to have no written constitution. Ever since Ch'in Shih Hwang Ti overthrew the feudal states of Chou in 221 BC and drew all parts of the country under one central control, China has had a unitary system of government, as distinct from a federal system such as exists in USA. Supreme power has rested with the Imperial court and central government in the capital; the provinces have enjoyed no reserved rights such as are enjoyed by the individual states of USA. This is not to say that China has been a great monolithic structure. Clearly, given a country of this size, its viceroys and provincial governors have, of necessity, had considerable local autonomy and discretion in the application of rules and edicts issuing from the centre. This unitary pattern has continued to the present day. Under the new People's Constitution China is defined as a 'unified multi-national state'.

When the Communist forces swept southward in 1949 and so quickly obtained control of the whole country, they found it in a state of administrative chaos. In spite of the suddenness of victory, however, they were not entirely unprepared to meet the enormous governmental problems that faced them. A good deal of thought and training had gone into their sojourn in Yenan. In *The New Democracy*, which he wrote in 1949, Mao Tse-tung had envisaged a long period of co-operation with any and all progressive elements before achieving the socialist state which was his aim.

47

Not least of Mao's problems was the lack of trained government personnel. Large numbers of civil servants fled to Taiwan with the KMT and many of those who remained were of suspect loyalty. In September 1949 the Chinese People's Political Consultative Conference (CPPCC) met and adopted the Organic Law and Common programme of the new Central People's Government of the People's Republic of China. This body continued to function until 1954. The country was immediately divided into six large administrative regions: North China Central Control Area and five districts—North-East; East; Central South; North-West; South-West.

Elections to appoint deputies to the first National People's Congress (NPC) were held in 1953. These were on the basis of universal suffrage of all citizens of eighteen years and over. Only 'undesirable persons' (capitalists, landlords and members of KMT) were excluded from the franchise. Over 300 million people voted. Election of deputies is indirect, the rural districts (*hsiang*) and market towns (*chen*) electing their representatives to the districts (*ch'u*) and the districts in their turn, theirs to the counties (*hsien*), and so on through the provinces (*sheng*) to the NPC. Congresses are elected every four years.

The 1,226 deputies of the first NPC met on 15 September, 1954 and adopted the Constitution, declaring the Congress to be the highest organ of state in which all legislative, executive and judicial authority is vested. It has a Standing Committee, which functions when Congress is not sitting. The executive and administrative functions of government are carried out by the State Council. Mao Tse-tung was elected Chairman of the People's Republic of China, ie Head of State. His powers are great for he appoints and dismisses premier, vice-premiers and all important officers; he commands the armed forces, proclaims martial law and state of war. Mao held this office until 1959, when he resigned in favour of Liu Shao-ch'i, but he retained the chairmanship of the Chinese Communist Party (CCP).

The State Council is comprised of the Premier (Chou En-lai has held this post since 1954), Vice-Premiers, Secretary-General, Heads of Commissions and Ministers of nearly fifty

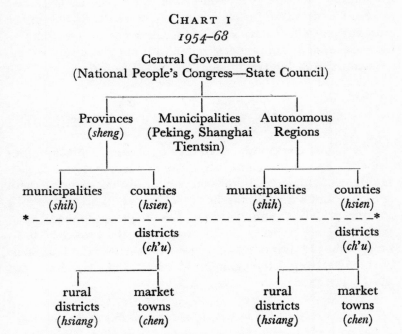

CHART I

1954–68

Central Government
(National People's Congress—State Council)

Provinces
(*sheng*)

Municipalities
(Peking, Shanghai
Tientsin)

Autonomous
Regions

municipalities
(*shih*)

counties
(*hsien*)

municipalities
(*shih*)

counties
(*hsien*)

districts
(*ch'u*)

districts
(*ch'u*)

rural
districts
(*hsiang*)

market
towns
(*chen*)

rural
districts
(*hsiang*)

market
towns
(*chen*)

* – – – – * Below this line, after 1958, many functions were performed by communes.

ministries, the most important of which are: Foreign Affairs, Internal Affairs, Agriculture and Forestry, Industry and Communications, Finance and Trade, Culture and Education, Justice, Minorities. The State Council is the executive and administrative body of the NPC, to whom it submits bills, and it co-ordinates the work of the ministries.

In 1954 the six large administrative districts, formed in 1949, were abolished and replaced by the old provincial areas of local government. The country is divided into provinces, autonomous regions, and municipalities directly under the central authorities below, which are the autonomous *chou*, counties, districts, rural districts and market towns. Each and all of these has its own local People's Congress and Council; each elects its representatives to the appropriate congress at higher level; each is responsible for the observance and execution of laws and decrees in its administrative area. Their respective functions and responsibilities have changed markedly with the changing political and economic pattern, eg with the formation of the communes and later with the Cultural Revolution.

CHINESE COMMUNIST PARTY

The above description has every appearance of that of an orthodox democratic constitution and so it is, but it is, of course, less than half the story. In the Chinese constitutional set-up there is throughout a dual hierarchy of Government and Communist Party at all levels. Although Mao Tse-tung had planned a long period of co-operation with all progressive elements, he left no doubt that the ultimate aim of government was the fulfilment of the objectives of the Communist Party. The Constitution of the CCP states:

During the period of transition from the founding of the People's Republic of China to the attainment of a socialist society, the fundamental task of the Party is to complete, step by step, the

———

A typical steppeland scene in the sheep, stock and horse rearing region of the Tsaidam in Chinghai.

Ship-building in China has increased enormously since 1949. The *Jing Song*, designed and built in China, is a 10,000 ton scoop-type suction dredger, fitted with the latest automatic devices, making it possible to load in 15 minutes. Many such dredgers are needed to keep the mouths of the Yangtze at Shanghai and the Hai-ho at Tangku open.

*socialist transformation of agriculture, handicrafts, capitalist
industry and commerce and to bring about, step by step, the industrialisation of the country.*

The CCP was founded on 1 July 1921 in Shanghai. Membership rose very rapidly during the years of partnership with
KMT, 1924–7, to 58,000. Numbers fell very severely during the
Long March but by 1945 membership was reported to be
1,210,000. During the next ten years numbers rose steadily and
rapidly. The last figures published were those of the year of the
Great Leap Forward, 1959—13,960,000. An estimate made in
1965, just before the Cultural Revolution, placed membership
at about 18 million. Membership of the Party is considered an
honour and a privilege, demanding deep dedication and
loyalty to the cause. Members are subject to the most rigid
discipline and continuous education in current thought on
Communist ideology and on the Party Line. In this way a
unified body, fired with revolutionary fervour has been built up.
Through its cadres, ie its members thus trained, it permeates
and influences every walk of life, not only government offices
at all levels but factory, school, hospital, hamlet and every
army unit. The influence and teaching of the Party are ex-

Chairman Mao Tse-tung and Premier Chou En-lai enjoying a
firework display in Tien An Men Square, Peking, on National
Day, 1 October.

Commune members at the beautiful Temple of Heaven
celebrating, on 1 October 1971, the 22nd anniversary of the
founding of the People's Republic of China. All palaces, temples
and parks reserved for the élite in Imperial days are now open
to the public and freely visited.

D

tended to the young people and children through youth organisations. Seniors, up to the age of 25, are catered for in the
Communist Youth League. Members undertake 'to popularise
actively and faithfully carry out Party policies' and it is from
their ranks that full adult membership is recruited. Children up
to the age of 15 are urged to join the Young Pioneers. The
ubiquitous red scarf, emblem of membership, testifies to the
vast membership of this corps; the nearest comparable movements in the West are the Boy Scouts and Girl Guides.
The Pioneers' slogan is 'Be prepared, struggle for the
cause of Communism' and their reply 'Always be prepared';
their working style is 'Honesty, courage, vivacity and
unity'.

The organisational structure of the CCP is similar to that of
the National People's Congress. The Party holds periodic
national congresses, the last, the Ninth, being held in 1969.
Delegates are appointed by indirect election by Party congresses at all levels from factory, mine, commune and hsiang
upwards. All upper bodies are specifically enjoined 'to pay
constant heed to the views of their lower organisations'. The
National Party Congress elects a Chairman and a Central Committee for a term of five years. The Chairman appoints Vice-
Chairmen and the Central Committee elects the Politburo,
the Standing Committee and the Secretariat. Party organisations in the PLA take their instructions from the Central
Committee. Although the People's Constitution gives no
specific power or authority to the CCP, it nevertheless is the
undisputed power in the land. In fact, all the important
government posts are filled from the ranks of the Party's
Central Committee. More than a quarter of the Central Committee of the Eighth National Party Congress consisted of
Ministers and Vice-Ministers.

During the thirteen years between the Long March and
Liberation the Communists, from their base in Yenan, Shensi,
experimented and gained experience in government. The hardships of the march and the bitter experiences of the war years
served to forge a bond of comradeship and unity, which held

firm during the first ten years of power. When the NPC in 1954 elected Mao as Chairman, he had for his Vice-Chairmen Liu Shao Ch'i, Chou En-lai, Chu Teh and Ch'in Yu, all veterans who had been through fire with him. Lin Piao was added late in 1958. It was not until 1959 as the Great Leap Forward developed and the communes were formed that deep-rooted differences and 'contradictions' in approach to socialism began to make their appearance in the ranks of leadership. These differences were eventually to break out into open opposition in the Cultural Revolution in 1966.

THE GREAT LEAP FORWARD

Synchronising with the revolutionary changes in agricultural organisation brought about by the formation of the communes in 1958, a similar upheaval took place in the industrial field. Amid tremendous enthusiasm the country embarked on a campaign 'to achieve communism in our time' and in a decade to turn China into a modern industrial state. In many communes an attempt was made immediately to give effect to the socialist ideal of 'from each according to his ability, to each according to his need'. Free communal kitchens were formed, peasants' private plots and free markets were abolished. Needless to say, so sudden an introduction of such revolutionary ideas into a peasant economy, which is essentially conservative, met with some opposition, especially to the loss of private plots, and the more radical innovations were quickly dropped.

On the industrial side targets were set for the increase of production in virtually all commodities but attention was concentrated mainly on iron and steel. Great Britain's steel production was to be equalled and overtaken in a couple of years. The whole programme was embarked upon with great fervour and energy. Peasants forsook their fields to build little blast furnaces on any handy piece of waste land. Iron ore of almost any quality was collected and transported to these furnaces, largely on foot by carrying-pole. Pig iron production sprang from 5,860,000 metric tons in 1957 to a reported 12,700,000 metric tons in 1960. Similar, although not so spectacular, increases were reported in coal, electric power, cotton and many other commodities. 1958 was a year of bumper crops but, unfortunately, they were not fully harvested because much farm labour was diverted to industrial work, particularly 'backyard' iron smelting. It was a year of great optimism, euphoria and self-sacrifice. Boys and girls, young men and young women formed themselves into brigades and battalions and marched out to work with banners flying and bugles blowing, and performed prodigious tasks of endurance. Communes, brigades, production teams, factories and mines, in their enthusiasm, vied with each other in setting themselves higher and yet higher targets of production—too often impossible of attainment. So appeared one of the early casualties of this fantastic year. Either lack of competent clerical records or failure to reach the promised target led to unreliable or false returns. The State Statistical Bureau, which during the previous six to eight years had been slowly and laboriously built into a reliable professional organ, collapsed. Since 1959 it has ceased to publish hard figures and has reverted to the use of percentages. Other casualties were under and over production of various commodities and bottlenecks in both production and transport with their resultant chaos.

It was disagreement within the CCP over the rightness of this Great Leap which first revealed the break in unity of the Politburo. Those who, led by Mao, supported the Leap, held that 'redness', ie correct ideological thought and dedication, were the *sine qua non* of the Revolution and that such outbursts as this were essential to the constant renewal of the revolutionary spirit particularly amongst the younger generation. Those opposed to this approach, led by Liu Shao-ch'i, Po I-po (Director of Industry and Commerce) and Li Fu-chun (Planning Commission), advocated a more orthodox development of industry by professional expertise and wage incentives. Defence Minister P'eng Teh-huai was the first notable victim of this tension, which was felt in army circles no less than elsewhere. P'eng Teh-huai, most capable and forceful of CCP military commanders, had been with Mao throughout the Long March. After his experiences as Commander-in-Chief of the Chinese volunteers in Korea in 1950–1, when his forces were very dependent on USSR for military material, he strongly advocated greater professionalism within the army, less 'politics in command' and less involvement of the PLA in civilian labour, while Mao was wedded to the old army pattern evolved during the Sino-Japanese war. In 1959 P'eng and his staff were dismissed and replaced by Lin Piao, who signalled his appointment by abolishing all ensignia of rank in the army.

The years 1959 to 1961 were marked by serious drought and disastrous harvests, which, in former years, would have resulted in widespread famine. Thanks to the improvements in transport during the previous ten years making distribution possible and also to strict food rationing, which followed the British pattern of World War II, calamity was averted. There was some malnutrition but no starvation. There followed a big reversal in economic policy in that agriculture, instead of industry, was put 'in command'. Whereas, in the previous ten years, industry had been receiving about 60 per cent of the country's capital investment as against agriculture's 7–8 per cent, emphasis was now placed on agricultural development and industry was ordered to serve it by providing more agricultural machinery, tractors, tools and fertiliser.

Due partly to the economic disorganisation caused by the Great Leap and partly to the sudden withdrawal of all technical aid from Russia, 1959–61 were lean years also for industry. However, the considerable capital investment made during those years began to bear fruit in 1962. A marked change in policy emerged, which developed into what came to be known as the New Economic Policy. In agriculture private plots were restored to the peasants, who were again able to engage in side-line production, which could be sold on the free market. In the industrial field 'expertness' assumed greater importance than 'redness'. Managerial staff and the technocrats took command; the criterion of success of a concern was its ability to make a profit; in factories, the incentives to greater effort offered to workers were differentials in wages and bonuses in many forms. Inevitably bureaucracy increased and there developed within factories hierarchies with élite or privileged groups at their heads. The NEP was clearly leading both industry and agriculture into paths which were anathema to Mao Tse-tung. The reliance on the profit motive and bonuses—Economism and 'taking the capitalist road', as he dubbed it—if allowed to get entrenched would defeat all his efforts to promote the moral motivation of unselfish service of the masses. The stage was therefore set for a struggle not only for leadership of the Party but also to determine which of these two divergent roads was to be followed.

THE GREAT PROLETARIAN CULTURAL REVOLUTION

Mao's first attacks were directed in 1964 against the literary and artistic circles, alleging their long continued subversive and 'revisionist' writings and their alienation from the workers and peasants. In autumn 1964 a socialist education campaign was started under the slogan *si ching* or Four Clean Ups. During the next two years these criticisms increased; in 1965 the Shanghai Party Committee attacked the Peking Party Committee, alleging rightist sympathies. These attacks resulted in the dismissal of P'eng Chen, Mayor of Peking, but the full fury of the Cultural Revolution was not released against the 'revisionists', 'élitists' and 'capital roaders' until June 1966. The occasion was a demonstration by Peking University students protesting against 'élitism' in education. The university walls were plastered with wall newspapers attacking the reservation of university and school places for the élite and privileged, ie the Party leaders and industrial management, and demanding more for workers and peasants. Party cadres, sent in to resolve the difficulties, failed signally. The protest spread spontaneously to schools throughout the city and then throughout the country. Walls everywhere were covered with *ta-tzu-pao*, big-character newspapers, proclaiming the views and ideas of individuals and groups and inveighing against all kinds of ills.

Mao was quick to utilise this upsurge of feeling. On 6 August 1966 he issued his 'Sixteen Points'. (A great deal of government during the ensuing years was done by such directives.) These contained much of what he had preached before but they had added point in the circumstances: revolution is right and good; put your trust in the masses; have courage to speak out and to criticise but rely on discussion and not on force; break down old tradition and build the new. He praised the use of wall news-papers as a good way of carrying on debate. Students (from about the age of 12 upward) concentrated on Peking from all parts of the country. They were given free transport, free meals and accommodation. On 18 August 1966 a great rally was held in the square at T'ien An Men at which Mao, amid scenes of tremendous enthusiasm, officially inaugurated the Red Guards and conferred on them their red arm-bands. These Red Guards, for a while, were given great freedom and exer-cised great power within the city. It is not surprising, given their youth and the exhortation to rebel and criticise, that there were a good many excesses, such as the wrecking of museums in which there were exhibitions of old culture and the attack on people whose dress or manner did not conform to what a par-ticular group thought was correct. One group of Red Guards in their criticism of another sometimes came to blows. By the end of the year a halt was called to the influx of Red Guards, all anxious to get at least a glimpse of Chairman Mao. The strain on transport, accommodation and feelings demanded relief. The Red Guards were urged to take to their feet and emulate the veterans of the Long March, taste and learn from hardship and bitterness and, armed with *Quotations from Chairman Mao Tse-tung*, spread the gospel far and wide.

The fight between the two opposing groups within the Party was now fully joined. At the beginning of 1967 the Maoists turned their whole forces against 'the handful of persons within the Party who are in authority and taking the capitalist road' and in particular against Liu Shao-ch'i, who was dubbed

'China's Khrushchev'. Revolutionary committees were formed and, joined by Red Guards, entered factories and government offices demanding an end to economism, élitism and bureaucracy. The rationalist NEP group, led by Liu, responded by an intensification of their incentives in the hope of retaining the loyalty of the workers by increasing bonuses of all kinds. The struggle was bitter and sometimes resulted in violence and bloodshed. The PLA, whose loyalty was not always crystal clear, as evidenced in the incidents in Wuhan and Canton, was called in to keep the peace. By the end of 1967 Mao was victorious. Liu Shao-ch'i, Chief of State and for long regarded as Mao's heir was, degraded, together with many other leading figures, notably T'eng Hsiao-ping, General Secretary, and Po I-po, Minister of Industry and Communication. It should be noted that the purge, although ruthless, was not accompanied by physical elimination. Elimination has not the same physical connotation in Chinese as it has in the West. The Ninth Party Congress in 1969 annulled the old Party constitution and adopted a new one in which Lin Piao was named heir-apparent. Few of the old guard were left.

This power struggle within the Party and the purging and degrading of so many of its leading figures could not but bring discredit on the CCP. For a while it lost much of its power and has regained it only slowly following an intensive Party rectification campaign (struggle-criticism-transformation). It is now largely in the hands of the younger generation of energetic and idealistic cadres but emphatically under Mao's leadership.

While the form of government at the centre remained largely undisturbed, provincial government underwent a big change. As the provinces one by one came more firmly under Mao's control, so they developed Three-way Alliance Revolutionary Committees, a pattern of government first formed in Heilungkiang in 1967. These committees are made up of representatives drawn from the revolutionary cadres, from the revolutionary masses and from the PLA. No rigid proportion between the three partners is laid down but, in practice, the PLA representation is in the majority and, almost invariably a military man is chairman. Below the Provincial committees similarly composed Revolutionary Committees are to be found at all levels of local government—in communes, market towns and factories.

The government of the country since 1949 has hinged very largely on the leadership of Mao Tse-tung. As he has become older so has the question of succession increased in importance. In the 1950s and early 1960s Liu Shao-ch'i was regarded as the Chairman Elect. His conflict with Mao after the Great Leap Forward and during the New Economic Policy between 1961 and 1964 led to his being demoted at the beginning of the GPCR in 1966. Lin Piao, Defence Minister, was nominated by Mao as his successor and appeared at Mao's right hand at all

CHART 2
After Cultural Revolution

Central Government
(NPC   State Council–Politburo   PLA)
|
Provincial Three-way Alliance Revolutionary Committees
(Revolutionary Cadres   Revolutionary Masses   PLA)
|
| Revolutionary Committees at all levels |
(counties, municipalities, districts, communes)

official functions until September 1971, when it was announced that Lin Piao and several high-ranking military and air force officers had been killed in an air crash in Mongolia. The incident assumed greater significance when all unsold copies of *Quotations from Chairman Mao Tse-tung* were recalled and Lin Piao's preface expunged.

It was not until July 1972 that an official announcement was made, declaring that an attempt on Mao's life had been made, that a coup d'état, led by Lin Piao and senior officers, had been foiled and that they had died while attempting to escape. The entire air force was grounded and extensive purges of senior officers in the forces carried out. General Yeh Chien-yin was recalled from retirement to take the post of Defence Minister. At the time of writing Mao's successor is still unnamed.

THE NATIONAL MINORITIES

Special constitutional arrangements are made for the government of the various national minorities within the People's Republic. There are more than fifty of these, located mainly on the borders of China Proper and occupying more than 60 per cent of the whole of China. At the 1954 census they numbered over 35 million; today the figure is probably about 43 million.

The minorities are given self-governing status under the Standing Committee of the NPC according to their greatly varying stages of development. For example, there are the very primitive Kutsung people, numbering between 2,000 to 3,000, who live in the forests of south Yunnan on the Vietnam border. They are gatherers and hunters, clothed in leaves and hides, with lean-to shacks of boughs and banana leaves for housing; they have no written language. They are now being settled, the men learning to grow cotton, vegetables and fruit and the women to spin and weave. Chinese authorities claim that the transition to Communism for them was easy since they were still in the stage of 'primitive communism' in which class society had not yet developed. In contrast to the Kutsung of the south there are the Olunchins of Inner Mongolia, fur trappers of reindeer, boar and squirrel in the Ta Kingan Mountains. They also number about 3,000 and are now settled.

Most of the smaller nationalities are located in south-west China. In Yunnan alone there are twenty-one—more than in any other province. They include Yi, Tai, Miao, Pai, Wu, Tibet, Lahu, Lisu, Hani, Tulung, Penglung and Pulang, and they number 6 million or one-third of the population of the province.

There are five Autonomous Regions. These are the Sinkiang Uighur AR, Ningsia Hui AR, Tibet AR, Kwangsi Chuang

AR, and Inner Mongolia AR. Some of these *chou* now have greatly increased Han (Chinese) population due to immigration. For example, the Uighur population in Sinkiang in 1954 was 3,640,125. Since then more than 2,000,000 young Chinese have moved into the region. In addition to the *chou* there are 54 autonomous counties (*hsien*) and 269 districts (*ch'u*) and municipalities (*shih*).

In order to train acceptable leaders, cadres, teachers and technicians, Institutes of National Minorities have been opened. That in Peking now accommodates 2,600 students of 47 different nationalities, including 900 Tibetans. When the writer visited it in 1956 it contained a Muslim mosque and a Buddhist temple. It was at that time directed by one of China's outstanding sociologists, Fei Hsiao-t'ung. There are now eight such institutes in China.

CURRENCY AND BANKING

We have noted the chaotic state of the currency at the time of Liberation in 1949. It was generally anticipated abroad that financial and economic difficulties would quickly bring the young People's Republic to its knees. The Korean War in 1950 and USA blockade and embargo on Chinese goods did nothing to lessen the strain and burden. How then was it that, against all expectations, within a matter of two years galloping inflation was brought to a standstill and the currency achieved a stability which has been maintained over the succeeding twenty years, unmatched by any other country in the world?

Among the main measures was the immediate confiscation of all 'bureaucratic capital and enterprises', ie all concerns, governmental and private in the hands of the KMT. Much of this material had been held for speculation on the unstable market. By strict administration of the market this speculation was stopped. The shuttling of grain and goods from surplus to deficiency areas also helped. Very important was the institution of a unified, efficient tax collection; the severest penalties for corruption and bribery were imposed with a result that all taxes flowed into the national treasury instead of seeping away into hundreds of illegal channels. But most important of all measures was the establishment of a state bank to control the financial market and regulate the volume of currency in circulation. All the big KMT 'bureaucratic capitalist' banks were confiscated. The smaller privately owned banks were gradually absorbed in the Joint State-Private Bank system. The People's Bank of China, which had been founded by the Communists in 1948, was made directly responsible to the State Council Office of Finance and Trade. It has the sole right to issue notes and coin (Jenminpi-Yuan), which are the only legal tender and it has the duty of maintaining the correct balance between money in circulation and consumer goods. This it does without any legal limit being placed on the amount it issues. As essential difference between the situation in China and in USA and UK is that in China all industrial and co-operative transactions are carried through by bank transfers, whilst cash is used almost entirely for the payment of wages and individual personal purchases. The People's Bank of China keeps all government accounts. It has branches in every *hsien* in the country and every unit in the army, and every co-operative has to bank with it. Other banks are subordinate to the People's Bank. For example, the Bank of China handles foreign business and overseas remittances. It has branches abroad, notably in Hong Kong, where it stands alongside the Hong Kong and Shanghai Bank and the Chartered Bank. The sixty or seventy private banks which were gathered into the Joint State-Private Bank in 1949–50 handle savings deposits, which have grown to considerable proportions in the last twenty years. The financing of state farms, communes, co-ops and big loans needed for works like water conservancy is done by the Agricultural Bank of China. A like function for industry is done by the People's Construction Bank of China.

Foreign banks disappeared very quickly after Liberation with the exception of the Hong Kong and Shanghai and Chartered Banks, which each have a branch in Shanghai but whose work is concerned solely with financing foreign trade. Foreign exchange rates vary with the status of the country. There are two rates for socialist countries: one, the official quotation for trading transactions, fixed at present for only Russian roubles (100 roubles to 222.22 JMP yuan) and Rumanian leis (100 leis to 33.33 JMP yuan); the other, the non-trade quotation covering such expenditure as embassy expenses, delegations, students. These are very favourable: 100 roubles to 129 JMP and 100 leis to 15.54 JMP. For capitalist countries, buying and selling rates are quoted through the People's Bank of China. The sterling rate in 1965 for £1 was: buying rate 6.85 JMP yuan and selling rate 6.92 JMP yuan. Since there were no legal trade transactions with USA, no rates are quoted.

TAXATION

Unlike both USA and UK, China derives none of its revenue from direct taxation of individual income. There is no tax on salaries or wages or on interest from government bonds. What is called Industrial and Commercial Income Tax is levied on net profits of non-state enterprises but as few of these concerns still exist, it provides very little revenue. However, absence of income tax does not mean absence of taxation. In order to obtain the capital necessary for all the development that is taking place vast sums must be raised and this is done mainly by taxation at source. All state enterprises pay their profits into the state treasury and it is from these profits that the central government derives more than two-thirds of its annual income. All state enterprises, in the last resort, are under central authority, which can, by price control, manipulate this form of taxation.

Most of the other third of the national revenue comes from agriculture. The Agricultural Tax is levied on all the produce of the commune, production brigade and production team and is based on a 'normal yield', which, it is claimed, is calculated well below the actual yield. The rate was set by the State

Council in 1958 and varied between 13 per cent and 19 per
cent according to the province. Newly developed land is given
total exemption. In addition the communes and co-operatives
are required to sell surplus grain to the state at prices fixed by
the state according to quality and variety. These prices have
varied considerably with changes in government policy. Prices
in general have been below those of the free market.

Other taxes of minor importance are the Salt Tax, which in
the old days was greatly hated but was a great money spinner
for the collectors. Today it accounts for less than 2 per cent of
the revenue. Customs duties, which are unnecessary in a
socialist regime from a protectionist standpoint, are retained as
a bargaining counter in foreign trade transactions. Vehicles,
bicycles and boats are all required to be licensed and a road tax
is levied on some cars and carts.

JUSTICE

In old China, unless you had a fat purse and a friend at
court, you were ill-advised to go anywhere near the law courts,
such was their reputation for fiddle, bribery and corruption.
For the poor, litigation spelt certain disaster.

The Constitution of 1954 abolished the judicial system and
legal code of the KMT. It declared that every citizen, regardless
of status, race, sex or creed, enjoyed equality before the law.
Except in the reform of marriage laws, no fully developed code
of law has been achieved. Legal enactments reveal the same
lack of precision that is characteristic of so many government
regulations and 'instructions'. It may be that this is deliberate
and embodies the old concept, which held that right behaviour
(*li*) was the proper basis for judgement rather than legal enact-
ment (*fa*), in some ways similar to common law in medieval
England. Lack of a well-defined legal system was one of the
criticisms that the intelligentsia levelled against the Communists in 1957 during the 'hundred flowers' outburst. However, whatever shortcomings there are, there can be no doubt

that the common man has a much greater chance of justice and a fair deal than ever before.

The Judiciary is declared by the Constitution to be independent of the Executive and subject only to law. The Supreme People's Court is the highest in the land; its president is appointed for four years as are also the presidents of the local, intermediate and special courts. There is a right of appeal from a lower to a higher court. Mrs Shih Liang, Minister of Justice, reported in 1957 that there were only some 2,000 lawyers trained in the new legal procedure, which is simple. Courtrooms are bare and unpretentious; procedure lacks the intimidating atmosphere found in some of our Western courts. Judicial proceedings in the people's intermediate and local courts make use of a system of people's assessors—a sort of panel of lay judges, who are elected, any citizen being eligible. In 1957 there were 246,500 assessors from all walks of life, workers, peasants, clerks, industrialists and businessmen. Cases are heard by one judge and two assessors with equal voice in judgement.

The object of all imprisonment is the reformation of the offender and his return to society as a good citizen. The first step in this process, it is held, is to obtain from the prisoner a recognition of his fault and a confession of his guilt. Great faith is placed in reform through labour and through constant study of the *Thoughts of Mao Tse-tung*. All crimes (theft, embezzlement, crimes of violence) strictly speaking are crimes against the state but the really heinous ones are those of counterrevolution aimed at the overthrow of the Communist regime. Reform from this may be hard and long in one of the State Reform Farms. It would appear from the reports of visiting foreigners that many are open prisons where there is little or no visible restraint, from which the prisoners go out daily to work and to which they return at night. Some prisons even have factories within their walls. The prisoners receive no wages— only pocket money—but have holidays when they can visit relatives. It is worth noting that the problem of unpaid labour competing with outside industry does not arise in China as it does in Western Europe and USA.

Law and order are maintained very largely through a modification of the old *pao chia* system by which every group of ten households was held responsible for the behaviour of its own members. Today everyone is a member of some group or other in factory, school, office, production team, each with its own security committee. It is through these that considerable psychological and social, rather than physical, pressure is exerted to maintain Communist puritan tenets of behaviour. This is the main reason why police are so little in evidence except for traffic control in the cities. The fact that the peasant and worker militia throughout the country are armed with rifles testifies that the vast majority acquiesce in this form of control.

PEOPLE'S LIBERATION ARMY (PLA)

The earliest CCP military force was that which formed part of Chiang Kai-shek's Northern Expedition in 1926. In 1927 the KMT and CCP split and became bitter enemies. Between 1928 and 1934 Mao and Chu Teh steadily built up an army, composed entirely of volunteers, based in the mountainous country round Chingkangshan, Hunan. Here they steadily resisted all Chiang's attempts to oust them until in 1934 they were forced to retreat. The Long March, vividly described by Edgar Snow in *Red Star over China*, eventually landed them in October 1935 in Yenan, Shensi. During all this time Mao devoted much of his thought and energy to the inculcation of basic Communist ideology into his rugged forces. He insisted on rigid discipline, which included strict rules for honest and humane treatment of the peasants, a factor which stood the army in good stead in subsequent campaigns. This indoctrination continued and was stepped up during the struggle against Japan, so that when in 1949 KMT resistance collapsed, the army which surged south was not only a highly disciplined but also a dedicated Communist missionary force. One personal incident must suffice to illustrate the spirit that permeated the PLA. In summer 1949 when the PLA took Wuhan without resistance, a company occupied the campus of the Central China University. They stacked their (American) rifles, captured from the KMT, and immediately began preaching their Marxian gospel to the students. Their arms were spick and span; their uniforms, although rather threadbare, were clean and their behaviour exemplary. In the days that followed they started cultivating any reasonable (sometimes unreasonable) piece of wasteland, setting an example which was followed by many of the students.

Large numbers of the PLA were demobilised after Liberation. Very many of them were formed into Construction Corps, which settled, developed and farmed frontier lands, notably Sinkiang and Heilungkiang, thus killing several birds with one stone. Employment problems of demobilisation were relieved; vulnerable USSR border lands were occupied by increased numbers of reliable Han people; production was increased.

Conscription was not adopted until 1954; all citizens between the ages of 18 and 40 are liable for service, the length of which varies—Army 3 years, Air Force 4 years, Navy 5 years. Since only some $2\frac{1}{2}$ million men are required for the forces, only the physically and mentally fit and the literate are chosen. Selection for service is regarded as an honour and moreover it provides an entry later into higher social service.

As we have seen, the PLA during the Cultural Revolution was repeatedly called on to perform the difficult and often unenviable job of keeping the peace between contending factions. It is, therefore, not suprising that in the subsequent formation of Provincial Revolutionary Committees the major representation was assigned to the PLA.

4

How They Live and Work in the Country

THE old social scale of imperial China ran, in descending order, thus: the landed gentry, from whom the scholar-administrator sprang; the peasant farmer; the handicraftsman; the merchant; the soldier and criminal. At first blush this may be a surprise to the Westerner until it is remembered that four-fifths of the population lived and still live in the country in half a million villages. The type of settlement varies with the region and the density of population, ranging from large villages of up to 2,000 inhabitants through hamlets, often composed of one extended family (eg Chu Chia Wan—the hamlet of the family of Chu) to isolated homesteads.

Great changes have taken place in the last twenty years in rural life. In order to appreciate the extent of these changes some account of the state of the peasantry before 1949 is essential. Population, which had remained remarkably static since Han times (202 BC), showed startling increase during the Ch'ing (Manchu) dynasty, particularly from the middle of the eighteenth century. With this increase came a steady growth of land hunger as inheritances were divided. This became acute at the turn of this century. Peasants' holdings became smaller; the average size of farm in the wheat-growing north was 7·5 acres and in the rice-growing south 2–3 acres. Rents, whether fixed on a share or crop basis, were increasingly oppressive, the landlord rarely taking less than half the harvest. Absentee landlordism increased and, with it, landlord oppression. Poor communications and lack of knowledge of the market made exploitation by the middleman easy. Poor credit facilities and the inescapable social demands of celebrations at birth, marriage and death drove the peasant into the hands of the moneylender, who, more often than not, was his own landlord. Interest rates were seldom less than 2 per cent per month; far more often over 100 per cent per annum. In this way the wretched peasant often fell deeply into debt and lost any right to his land or tenancy and became landless. To add to his misery, especially during the war-lord period (1915–27), taxation pressed very heavily and was sometimes collected years ahead. When drought or flood came he ate bitterness (*ch'i k'u*) to the full and was often forced to sell his children to save them from starvation. The plight of the peasant in the years 1920–30 is fully discussed in R. H. Tawney's *Land and Labour in China.*

When the victorious Northern Expedition swept aside war-lord Wu Pei-fu's troops in 1926, they did so largely on Sun Yat-sen's slogan and promise of 'Land to the Tiller', which gained the ready support of the peasant. Chiang Kai-shek failed to implement this promise. The Communists in 1949, using the same battlecry, defeated Chiang and immediately started to put their land reform programme into practice.

LAND REFORM AND CO-OPERATIVES

The CCP has always proclaimed that 'the fundamental task of the Party is to complete, step by step, the social transformation of agriculture, handicrafts and capitalist industry and commerce and to bring about, step by step, the industrialisation of the country'. Its first step in agriculture appeared to be in the opposite direction to socialisation. Between 1949 and 1951 land was taken from the landlords and rich peasants and re-distributed to those who cultivated it. This clearly meant increased fragmentation of the land and cultivation, in many instances, by less efficient farmers with a consequent fall in production. This the country could ill afford. The government, therefore, was quick to urge on the peasants a next step, which was that they should combine in small groups to form Mutual Aid Teams for cultivation. This directive was easily accepted by the peasants since it was much in line with what had been the practice over the centuries. Its advantages were obvious. In 1953 elementary Agricultural Producers Co-operatives were introduced. Individual peasants were persuaded to pool their land and tools and to work their combined plots together. Persuasion was the operative word; cadres were enjoined to avoid pressure and to develop the APCs gradually, step by step. The peasant retained his title to his land and had the right to withdraw. Each peasant received payment according to the work he put in and the capital (land, animals, carts, tools) he contributed. Since ownership of the land was retained, the scheme was fairly well received and it expanded rapidly. Nevertheless the working units achieved by the APCs were still not large enough to give satisfactory increase in production. In 1955 Advanced APCs (Collectives) were introduced in the belief that the larger the unit of both land and labour, the greater would be production. These Advanced APCs were much larger than the Elementary, embracing about 160 households or 600 persons. There was a good deal of opposition to this step since it involved the surrender of individual ownership of land; small plots for private cultivation were retained. Remuneration was increased by work points, ie according to work done and less for land contributed. In spite of opposition coming mainly from middle peasants, 752,000 APCs, of which 668,000 were advanced, had been formed by early 1958. They came under considerable criticism as being too large and bureaucratic and it appeared as though they were about to be reduced in size when, paradoxically, in April 1958 between 20 and 30 advanced co-operatives in Honan united and formed themselves into a commune.

COMMUNES

In the summer of 1958 Chairman Mao visited this experiment and declared it good. Within a matter of nine months the 700,000 co-operatives had been transformed into some 26,000 communes, each with an average of about 60,000 people. This was the rural contribution to the spontaneous outpouring of patriotic fervour and energy, which is known as the Great Leap Forward. The formation of the communes was carried through generally in China Proper amid much enthusiasm, although not entirely without misgiving and opposition. Their formation in the Autonomous Regions was carried out more gradually and with greater circumspection.

There were several underlying objectives in the formation of the communes. High among these was the hope of securing large and rapid continuing increase in agricultural production. There was also the intention in many minds of the rapid achievement of Communist society, which would give full expression to the principle of 'from each according to his ability, to each according to his need'. On the production side it was rightly held that the bigger unit of the commune would be able to carry out big works of land reclamation, irrigation and drainage, which were quite beyond the power of the smaller APC. Fuller use would be made of mechanisation and new agricultural techniques in fertilisation, pest control and seed selection. Moreover the unit would be big enough to 'walk on two legs' by building its own local road and rail communications, thus supplementing the main lines being expanded by the central authorities. It would also be able to develop small local industries and repair workshops. In this way it would assist the central government in its policy of devolution and relieve it to a large extent of capital expenditure, since the communes would be expected themselves to finance most of the above activities. It is in these fields that the communes have made their most valuable contribution during the last decade.

The communes took over the local government functions of the *hsiang* and much more besides. They were made responsible virtually for the entire life of their areas—for administration, agricultural and industrial production, finance, commerce, education, health, police and security (militia).

The description of a commune, which now follows, gives a general picture but it must be remembered that, while there is a pattern, in actual practice there is almost infinite variety. The individual performances and success of the communes have varied enormously, largely according to the quality of their leadership, the efficiency of their organisation and not a little to the quality of the soil they have to cultivate.

In the agricultural field the commune's main function is the over-all planning of production in accordance with the requirements of the State Planning Organisation. It also allocates, under provincial direction, the use of such capital funds as it has in irrigation and drainage works. This it has to balance against all the other industrial, educational and social claims made upon it. Work in the fields is the responsibility of production brigades and production teams. The brigade, more often than not, is identical with the village. It usually embraces about 100 families and an area of 150–70 acres. Its job is to organise and allocate the work of these families, who are divided into production teams of about 20 families apiece. The brigade does this by mutual agreement with the teams in village meetings. It will be seen that this method gives ample scope for debate and the airing of contradictions and their resolution. The brigade is also the accountancy body, being responsible for the distribution of consumer funds to the production teams after deducting Agricultural Tax, State Procurement charges (see Chapter 3, p 65) and local educational and social charges. The production teams are responsible for planning the actual work in the fields and producing the agreed quota of crops. They are given a considerable amount of freedom in this and much is left to their initiative. Over-production of the quota earns bonuses. Recent good harvests have led to nationwide debate over what proportion of this surplus should go to the individual consumer and what to greater investment in local industry, fertiliser and the like. Payment is by work points, usually estimated three times a year; after summer harvest, autumn harvest and a final distribution at the end of the year. A general estimate is that a peasant gets about 80 per cent of his income from collective work and 20 per cent from his private plot, side lines and savings in the credit co-op. Since production teams, even within one commune, work land of different fertility their shares in the income from collective work will vary. Brigades are constantly exhorted to make some rectification in this inequality.

The following table taken from the *Peking Review*, March 1966, gives distribution figures of Paching Production Brigade in 1964:

Production expenses	38·6 per cent	(seed, fertiliser, tractor hire etc)
Agricultural tax	6·5 per cent	
Reserve Fund	5·0 per cent	(new tools, livestock, improvements)
Welfare Fund	1·0 per cent	usually 3 per cent (sickness, old age)
Reserve grain	4·4 per cent	(against disaster)
Distributed to members	44·5 per cent	usually 50 per cent—bad weather divided according to work points—30–40 per cent in kind

There was considerable opposition to communes in those areas where enthusiasts tried to impose thorough-going Communism overnight. The abolition of private plots was particularly resented and there was a marked falling off of production in consequence. They were, therefore, quickly restored to private ownership but have been a continuing source of contention between Communist and individualist, the individualistic peasant being accused of devoting a disproportionate amount of time and manure to his own plot to the detriment of the team. Undoubtedly the private plots have been very productive in raising pigs, poultry and vegetables. Great exception was also taken where too great an attempt was made to communalise private life. For example, communal kitchens were set up where all had to feed—in some places meals were served free to all regardless of work done. It was not long before old habits were re-established, although communal restaurants are therefore used by those who desire them. Shortlived also were attempts to regiment life by housing youths and girls in dormitories in an endeavour to raise production. It was probably these excursions that gave rise to the widespread reports in the West of the Communists' desire to disrupt family life.

During and since the Cultural Revolution the commune has relinquished much of its power in the agricultural field. This has passed to the brigade and production team. It has, however, increasingly concerned itself with local industry. Medium-sized blast furnaces, heirs of the Great Leap, form the basis of local production of agricultural tools and machinery in many communes. Small- and medium-sized chemical plants produce fertiliser using local raw materials, thus saving transport.

HEALTH SERVICES AND WELFARE WORK IN THE COUNTRYSIDE

In the early part of this century such Western medicine as there was in the rural areas was in the hands of Christian missions, who had hospitals in many of the larger market towns. Country folk within reasonable distance could attend the hospital clinics. This service, although devoted, was very thinly spread. For the rest, the peasants had to rely on traditional Chinese medicine. Christian missions in this and in the educational sphere have had an influence out of all proportion to their numbers.

Immediately the People's Government came into power in 1949 a new approach was made. Emphasis was placed on the preventive rather than on the curative side of medicine. The normal six years doctor's training was cut to three, attention being concentrated on instruction in simple diagnosis, public health and hygiene, vaccination and inoculation. These doctors were sent out into the rural areas. Debilitating diseases like malaria, kala-azar, schistosomiasis and skin diseases, such as are endemic among rice-growers, came under attack. Education in public hygiene and cleanliness has been vigorously and successfully pursued. Anyone who has visited China and travelled on the railway will have been struck by the high standard, putting USA and UK to shame.

While, in recent years, the full six years' doctor's training has been resumed for work in hospitals and in the cities, emphasis is still laid on 'barefoot doctors' and mobile 'hospitals', whose services are now available in remote parts. No commune today is without its own efficient clinic. The effectiveness of this work is seen not only in the big drop in mortality rates especially among infants, but also in increased productiveness due to better health and energy. As a practical exercise of 'getting down from the horse and taking a look at the flowers' (see Chapter 2, p 43) town-based medical men and health workers are required to take part in tours of duty in the countryside.

Now that women are doing a great deal more than formerly both in the fields and in commune workshops, care of the young children has undergone a change. A great deal of this care rests in the hands of the old folk, especially the grandmothers, as it has in times past, but, today innumerable production teams and all brigades run their own crèches in which the very young are cared for while their parents are at work. Nearly everywhere in rural China the old people are taken care of in the family home. In the comparatively rare cases of old folk without family, they have the assurance through production team and brigade of the 'five guarantees' of adequate food, clothing, housing, medical care and honourable burial.

STATE FARMS

One of the agricultural objectives of the People's Government has been the rapid mechanisation of farming. This has not been easy of achievement in the small farms and small fields of China Proper but great strides have been made in the wide-open spaces of the north-east and north-west where state farms have been developed.

The great majority of these farms have been set up on marginal or waste lands, which, in the past, have remained undeveloped due to natural disabilities—drought-ridden or waterlogged, alkaline or acid soils, sand or wind bedevilled or too remote. Modern techniques, mainly of mechanisation, have enabled man to overcome these handicaps and vast areas have been brought into production. There are no recent statistics of number and size of state farms. Peking reported in 1961 that there were some 2,000 big state farms ranging from 5,000 to 250,000 acres. Most of China's output of tractors, combines etc in the early years went to the state farms. In spite of their size and their high output per man-hour, they produced only about 1 per cent of China's grain. State farms are distinguished from communes not only by their size, mechanisation and specialisation, but also by the fact that they are agricultural enterprises in the ownership of the whole people. Their profits go directly to the state and their workers are mainly on a wage basis.

Of the 710 state farms analysed in 1957, 361 were devoted to arable and 349 to livestock farming. Sinkiang had 102 farms, of which 58 were pastoral. Of Kwangtung's 87 farms, 81 were arable, while Inner Mongolia devoted 41 of its 46 farms to livestock. Heilungkiang, in the far north, had 42 arable and 15 livestock farms. State farms in the provinces of China Proper (notably Kwangtung, Kwangsi and Yunnan) are markedly smaller and more intensively farmed that those of the outlying lands. For example, the Pearl River State Farm in Kwangtung farms 4,500 acres of paddy rice. It claims that its output per acre is double that of communes in the vicinity with similar natural conditions.

The PLA has played a prominent part in the development of state farms. On the cessation of hostilities after Liberation large numbers of soldiers serving in Sinkiang and the North-East were demobilised and formed into Production and Construction Corps. They brought vast tracts of these outlying lands into production by irrigation and drainage and settled there with their families. The steady development of these frontier lands has encouraged further migration of Chinese and thus, to some extent, relieved the population problem. The call of patriotism and service for the people, together with the prospect of secure employment, has prompted young people to accept more willingly directed service in these remote regions.

EXPERIMENTAL AND DEMONSTRATION FARMS

In order to disseminate knowledge of new farming techniques and methods, experimental and demonstration farms have been set up all over the country. As their name indicates, the work of the experimental farms is to conduct tests on planting, sowing, seed strains, fertilisers, fish breeding, animal husbandry and farm management. They receive some financial help from the central government. The results of their work are passed onto innumerable demonstration farms whose job it is to test them further in their own local conditions and to popularise their findings among the brigades and production teams. These farms are organised and staffed, as a rule, by the communes and are assisted by some scientifically trained personnel. Some idea of how numerous they are can be gained from the fact that Hunan alone had 681 such stations in 1961.

AGRICULTURAL REGIONS

The above pages have sketched very briefly the stages of development and the general pattern of agricultural organisation since Liberation. It is now necessary to look more intimately at various regions in order to realise how very different the life and work of the peasant are in these parts. To do this effectively the reader is reminded of certain basic geographical facts (see Chapter 1, pp 16–18) which profoundly influence the whole pattern of life. A line drawn from Heilungkiang in the north-east to Yunnan at the Vietnam border roughly divides China of the highlands and plateaux from the great lowland river basins; the dry lands of the north-west from the wet lands of the south-east; the pastoralists from the arable farmers. The 15in isohyet closely follows this same line. Within the pastoralist area of the north-west, different altitudes of the various plateaux result in greatly differing ways of life.

LIFE AND WORK IN THE PLATEAUX REGIONS

Sinkiang Uighur Autonomous Region

The basin of the Tarim River is bounded on the south by the Kunlun Shan (Mountains), which form the northern edge of the Tibetan tableland. They are of great height, exceeding 20,000ft in many places, and are eternally snow-capped. The Tien Shan form the northern border of the basin and, although generally not quite as high as the Kunlun, support none the less great snowfields. The two mountain systems meet in the west in the Pamirs. From Charkhik in the east, through Yarkand, to Kashgar in the west innumerable rivers and streams flow down from the Kunlun and are lost eventually in the sands of the great Taklamakan desert, which occupies the centre of the basin. High up, below the snow line, nomadic pastoralists rear their flocks of sheep and goats. Communication with the lands below is difficult as the rivers descend in steep ravines. On these rivers, before they reach the desert and are lost in the sands, large oasis settlements have been in existence for many centuries. They have been sustained by careful irrigation, and since Liberation they have been given greater security by more modern and scientific methods, such as lining the irrigation channels and so preventing loss by seepage.

The rivers descending southward from the Tien Shan differ from those of the Kunlun in that they unite to form one river, the Tarim, which flows along the northern edge of the desert and is finally lost in the eastern sands around Lop Nor. These rivers from the Tien Shan also support oases. Famous towns have developed on these well-watered spots around the desert— Charcham, Khotan, Yarkand and Kashgar in the south and Kucha and Aksu in the north. It was along this ring of oasis towns that the old Imperial Silk Route and the Imperial Highway to Rome ran in Han times.

The oasis communities, who are Uighur in race, are now organised in communes. Their main food crops are wheat, maize, rice, kaoliang and barley; much fruit is also grown. A number of both arable and livestock state farms have been established, especially on the slopes of the Tien Shan.

The Turfan basin lies to the north-east of the Tarim basin. This is a remarkable depression, lying 940ft below sea level in the heart of this dry plateau. It is subject to great extremes of temperature, summer shade temperatures rising to 125°F (52°C) and falling below zero (−18°C) in winter. The Uighur farmers, who rely entirely on irrigation, produce fruit, cotton and grain. Turfan seedless grapes are famous. It is essential that every house has its dug-out, which provides a haven against the heat in summer and the cold in winter.

Dzungaria is the northern basin of Sinkiang, lying between the Tien Shan and Altai Mountains. For the most part it is a wide expanse of steppe and steppe-desert, occupied very sparsely by nomadic herdsmen. State farms on the northern slopes of Tien Shan and Bogdo Ula in the Manass and Kitai regions have considerably extended arable and pastoral farming. Life in this area has been revolutionised by the opening of the Karamai oilfield and the extension of the Lunghai railway from Lanchow to Manass.

Inner Mongolian Autonomous Region

Inner Mongolia forms the southern lip of the great Gobi desert depression and stretches from Sinkiang to Heilungkiang. It consists mainly of steppeland with some woodland on the north-facing slopes of the Nan Shan, Hara Karin Ula and Yin Shan but it becomes increasingly desert-like northward and westward. Like Sinkiang, Inner Mongolia is subject to great extremes of temperature, summer shade temperatures reaching 115°F (46°C) and winter −20°F (−29°C). Rainfall is sparse, precarious and liable to fall in violent hailstorms.

The grasses are tall and slender and are put to all sorts of use. The young tender shoots are fed to the livestock; the stalks serve the Mongolian as the bamboo does the Chinese and are put to all manner of domestic use—brushes, matting, kitchen utensils, bedding, curtains, toys, fences.

Where physical conditions are more favourable, eg along the northern stretch of the great bend of the Hwang-ho and in the oases of the Edsin Gol, population is settled and there are considerable towns, such as Huhehot the capital, Tsining, Wuchwan, and the great iron and steel city of Paotow.

Although the traditional way of life of the Mongolian is that of the nomadic pastoralist, he has tended to restrict his transhumance, that is, his seasonal movement of his flocks and herds, as far as possible. In consequence there has always been danger of overgrazing. He relies almost entirely on his flocks of sheep and goats for food—mutton, milk, cheese and butter. Brick tea from the Yangtze valley mixed with mutton broth forms his drink. His house must be portable and the yurt serves admirably. Its framework of willow canes and its cover of felt can be assembled and struck quickly by the womenfolk. It provides warm protection against the bitter winter winds and in summer the sides can be rolled up to allow free ventilation. In recent years plastics for the frame, cover and flooring are being increasingly used.

Since Liberation attention has been focused on turning these nomads into settled communities. To do this more than 20,000 wells have been sunk, ensuring adequate water for livestock and some irrigation for fodder crops. Co-operatives and later communes have been formed in which small industry such as meat-canning factories have been established.

The Tibetan Plateau

The greater part of the Tibetan plateau is so high and bleak as to be virtually uninhabited. At 16,000ft mean temperatures are −10°F (−23°C) in winter and rise to only 30°F (−1°C) in midsummer. There are two areas, Po and Chinghai, which have relatively dense population. Po is in the south-east corner where the Brahmaputra (Tsangpo) flows between the Himalayas and the Transhimalayas in a deep trough. It is here that the cities of Lhasa, Gyangtse and Shigatse are situated. After the expulsion of the Dalai Lama, a land reform campaign redistributed the feudal lands of lamaism and the peasants were organised into co-operatives. There has been extensive development of arable farming in the southern valleys and pastoral farming in the higher land to the north where some 7 million livestock are reared. The Tibetans are tea drinkers. Formerly brick tea was imported from Szechwan on the backs of coolies. It is now being grown locally.

Chinghai (Koko Nor), the large inland drainage lake, gives its name to the region of north-east Tibet. A large part of Chinghai is occupied by the Tsaidam basin, which lies between the Kunlun and Nan Shan. The centre of the basin is a vast swamp but the surrounding hills support good grass. The Tibetan pastoralists who live here and who, in past centuries, plagued travellers on the Imperial Highway running north of the Nan Shan, are famous for their horse breeding and for the fine quality of wool from their sheep and goats. This wool is worked into rugs and carpets at Sinning, the capital. The recent discoveries of coal seams over 100 feet thick near Tatsaitan, of good iron ore in the Nan Shan, of oilfields in both the centre and west of the Tsaidam and of immense deposits of salt near Chaka bid fair to change the whole way of life in Chingai within the next decade or two.

China's arable lands lie east and south of the pastoralist plateaux lands and virtually comprise what is known as China Proper. They stretch from 52°N to 18°N, from the Sungari and Nonni rivers of Heilungkiang to the tropical island of Hainan in the South China Sea, a distance of about 3,000 miles. Climates vary from the extremes of continental type in the north, through monsoon in the centre to tropical in the south. Within this vast area of approximately 2·1 million square miles lie the three great river basins of China, the Hwang-ho, the Yangtze Kiang and the Si Kiang. These arable lands contain nine-tenths of China's 750 million people. It will not be surprising to find that so great a region embraces big differences in types of farming and in ways of life.

The Chinling-Funiu Shan Axis

An axis of Hercynian folding, consisting of the Nan Shan in Kansu, the Chinling Shan in Shensi and Funiu Shan in

---

The Yangtze river bridge at Nanking is the third and latest to be built across the river since 1949. It is 6,700m (7,330yd) long and carries both road and rail transport. Note the paucity of cars compared with the numbers of cyclists and pedestrians. The photograph was taken in winter when the water is low.

Taching Oil Refinery in Heilungkiang province of the North-East is the most recent oilfield to be developed in China. The country's oil production is now considered adequate for her present needs.

Honan, stretches from east to west into Anhwei, dividing the country into two quite distinct regions. To the south the soils are leached and acid, rainfall is heavy, temperatures are warmer and more equable, the growing season is long, irrigation is widely practised and rice is the main crop. To the north, because rainfall is progressively lighter, soils are unleached and alkaline, greater and greater range of temperature is experienced, the growing season is short, and wheat, millet and kaoliang are farmed on dry lands for the most part.

South of the Axis

The way of life throughout the whole of the southern region has many similar characteristics. People everywhere are essentially rice farmers and consequently rice eaters. Rice farming is probably the most exacting of all forms of agriculture. Since it is cultivated best in flooded fields, it demands that those fields be absolutely level and the surrounding baulks carefully maintained. Except on the flattest of plains, this has necessitated careful terracing and accounts for the small fields, typical of south China hillsides. Water conservancy and irrigation are all important. Before Liberation when holdings were in individual

---

While table tennis holds sway among the younger generations, *hsiang-ch'i* (Chinese chess) is most popular among the elderly. These three are in an old people's home. Note the Chinese pipe with its small bowl and long stem; the Buddhist beads in the hand of the central figure; and the ball in the left hand of the player making the move, often used for rolling in the hand to keep fingers supple.

Action in Scene 2 of the ballet *The Red Detachment of Women*, first performed in May 1970. The purpose of all writing, opera and ballet in China today is to stimulate revolutionary fervour and to promote a spirit of 'service of the masses'.

F

hands, the equitable sharing of water was of utmost importance and was one of the liveliest subjects of discussion in every village and hamlet. Unauthorised deflection of water to one's own lands was a serious crime. This sharing called for a high degree of co-operation if farming was to be successful and this training over many centuries has paid dividends as socialisation of the land was carried through and co-operatives and communes formed. Irrigation demands much raising of water from the main channels to the fields. This has been done in the past by human labour laboriously working either treadle or hand-operated 'dragon skeleton' water wheels. These are steadily being replaced by either small diesel- or electric-powered pumps which can be carried from field to field and are proving a great boon both in saving labour and increasing production. There has been a phenomenal increase in the distribution of electric power lines in country districts during the last ten years.

Because the acid soils south of the axis are strongly leached by the heavy summer rains, adequate feeding is an urgent and constant problem. During the past twenty centuries fertility has been maintained by the regular application of night soil, which is carefully maturised in every village and hamlet. This, in times past, has been sufficient to maintain a balance between what is taken from the soil and what is put back but, with increasing population and growing demand for ever-greater production, the need for chemical fertiliser has become a first priority. Very many communes now have their own chemical fertiliser plant, which produces sufficient for their needs.

People everywhere in the south are rice eaters. Usually they have two main meals a day, at midday and in the evening, and also a light breakfast of *hsi fan* (rice gruel) or the 'left over' rice of the previous day. The amount of meat eaten is small and varies with the prosperity of the family, production team and brigade. It consists of pork, chicken or duck with some fish from river or pond. Generally speaking, however, vegetables (white cabbage, red broccoli, beans, peas, bean sprouts, bamboo shoots) and eggs provide the rice diet with variety.

In the far south (Kwangtung, Kwangsi, Hainan), where

there is a twelve-month growing season, two crops of rice a year are grown in the carefully terraced paddy fields. Between the harvesting of the autumn rice and the planting out of the spring rice the skilful farmer is able to take a catch crop of vegetables. Fruit growing (bananas, pineapples, mangoes, oranges, grapefruit) formerly received little attention but is now rapidly increasing in importance. Farther north, in the middle and lower basins of the Yangtze Kiang, where a short, sharp winter is experienced and summers are long and humid, the growing season is about ten months. There has been some double cropping of rice, especially in Hunan but, more generally, rice is grown in rotation with a winter crop of wheat, barley, beans or sweet potatoes. In the last ten years many large irrigation works have been carried out in this region, leading to a marked increase in double-cropping rice. This, together with the hillside of Fukien, is the great tea-growing region of China. Green tea is produced almost entirely for home consumption, while black tea serves both home and foreign markets. The coarser qualities are made up into bricks for export to Sinkiang, Inner Mongolia, Tibet and USSR. Cotton, ramie, hemp and tobacco are grown in Hunan and Hupeh. Chekiang and Anhwei produce a great deal of China's silk. The whole of the Yangtze valley is noted for its production of vegetable oils (rape, sesame and tea oil) and also *tung yu* (wood oil), which forms the basis of paints and varnish. Draught animals (water buffalo for the rice paddy and yellow oxen for the dry fields) are now being supplemented by tractors, notably the small 7hp walking tractor, which is very versatile and proving most useful in this type of farming.

Whilst there are hundreds of large market towns scattered throughout this southern region, the characteristic pattern of settlement is the village of less than 2,000 inhabitants, the hamlet and homestead. A typical hamlet would have a small grove of trees above it (propitiating the *feng shui*—wind and water spirits), five to ten houses, accommodating one or two extended families, and a pond in which some fish may be raised, draining into the rice fields below. The houses are probably either bamboo or timber framed with wattle and daub or sun-baked brick infill. Roofing is usually traditional Chinese tile or straw thatch. Cooking is done on the ubiquitous brick stove using wood, grass and any kind of root for fuel. This stove, probably more than any other factor apart from increasing population, has been responsible for deforestation in China. Conversion of the Chinese people to a coal-burning stove would be one of the main cures. No attention is given in the south to house heating and little even in the Yangtze basin. In winter padded cotton clothes are worn indoors and out-of-doors. A *ho-pen* or charcoal brazier is used in the more well-to-do homes.

Szechwan

Before we leave lands to the south of the Nan Shan-Chinling Axis, there is one province, Szechwan, which deserves individual attention. It is a vast land-locked basin of red sandstone of over 200,000 square miles, hemmed in by high mountain ranges. Its four large rivers, which give the province its name, drain into the Yangtze, which cuts its way out of the basin by the famous gorges on to the Hupeh plain. Throughout history Szechwan has been a natural stronghold. It was last put to the test when the Nationalists, under Chiang Kai-shek, retired there, set up their seat of government in Chunking and were able to defy their Japanese invaders until the end of the war in 1945.

Lying as it does in the heart of a landmass, one would expect Szechwan to experience great extremes of temperature between summer and winter but, owing to the high enclosing mountain ranges, the bitter out-flowing winter winds of Mongolia are deflected, and it enjoys a more equable climate than coastal regions of the same latitude (compare Chungking and Shanghai winter temperatures). This climate and a fertile soil enable the province to grow very nearly every crop of the entire country. It has the further distinction of containing one of the oldest irrigation systems in the world. Li Ping (255–206 BC), a famous Han engineer, tamed the torrents of the Min River, descending from the Chunghsia Shan on to the plain near present-day Chengtu, and converted a rock-strewn swamp into fertile land.

He did this by dividing and sub-dividing the river into innumberable channels, which today irrigate some 3,000 square miles of China's most fertile lands. Li Ping's slogan was 'Dig deep the channels; keep low the dykes', a principle which, if it could have been followed on the Hwang-ho, would have saved countless suffering. The system which Li Ping inaugurated has been maintained for over 2,000 years and today supports an agricultural population of nearly 2,000 persons to the square mile.

Another characteristic of Szechwan's climate is its cloudiness. There is a local saying which runs 'When the sun shines, the dogs bark', so rare is its appearance. The truth of the saying is emphasised by the name of the southern neighbouring province, Yunnan, which means 'South of the Clouds'.

North of the Axis

Between the two big arable regions of the rice farmers of the south and the wheat farmers of the north there lies a transitional belt in which the farmers are tempted to gamble on the chances of a big return by planting the heavier yielding and more valuable but riskier crop, rice, against the safer, but less lucrative, wheat. The risk lies, of course, in the fact that rainfall decreases steadily and becomes less and less reliable as one goes from south-east to north-west. Once well north of the Nan Shan-Chinling-Funiu divide and out on to the North China plain the risk is too great and very little rice is grown. Wheat, millet and kaoliang become the standard grain crops together with sweet potatoes. The latter are included in official grain statistics on a weight equivalent of 4: 1.

The climate of this northern arable area is characterised by its dry, bitterly cold winters and hot, comparatively wet summers. The winters become colder and longer and the summers drier the farther north and west one goes.

The following figures of mean monthly average temperature and total rainfall give some idea of the changes which take place.

Mean monthly average temperature

	January (°F)	July (°F)	Total rainfall (inches)
North			
Peking	23	79	24·9
Sian	33	86	13·8
Saratsi	5	73	13·5
Harbin	−2	72	21·5
South			
Canton	56	83	63·6
Hankow	40	85	49·6
Shanghai	38	80	45·2
Chungking	42	84	43·5

In the north the type of farming changes radically. Cultivation is almost entirely on dry fields. Any irrigation that has been carried out in the past on the plains has been by wells pumped either by manpower or by donkeys. Today, electric and diesel pumps are coming into increasing use. The growing period becomes steadily shorter towards north and west. On the North China plain it is approximately eight months and winters are not too severe to prevent the growth of winter wheat. On the higher lands of Shansi and Shensi the season is six months, permitting the growth of spring wheat only.

The whole area is subject to the dry bitterly cold northerly winds blowing out from the high pressure lying over the heart of Asia in winter. These winds are often heavily dust-laden, plaguing dwellers on the plains. In summer the whole pressure system is reversed. Moisture-laden south-easterly winds blow from the sea into the low pressure over the land during the summer. Approximately four-fifths of the rainfall falls between June and September. Its total is much less than in the south. Moreover, it is much less reliable. This unreliability, causing disastrous famines, has been responsible for the loss of countless millions of lives over the centuries. Happily, during the last twenty years increasing irrigation, modern farming techniques and vastly improved modern transport have mitigated, if not entirely removed, this threat.

Because rainfall in the north is so sparse, there is little or no leaching and all soils are alkaline, ie limey. The soils on the plains are a deep alluvium. The uplands of Shansi and Shensi are covered with loess, a fine wind-borne soil carried in from the desert lands to the north-west. This loess, in many places, is over 200ft thick. Given adequate moisture, it is very fertile. The soils of all these northern lands are in danger of alkalisation unless irrigation is carefully co-ordinated with drainage to carry off the rising accumulation of salts.

Houses on the plains are usually built facing south in order to get maximum benefit from the sun and to present their backs to the bitter winter winds. They are built of grey sun-baked brick and have thatched roofs of kaoliang stalks; often they have a surrounding wall enclosing a courtyard. Heating is by a central stove or *kang*, on which the family sleeps in the winter. In the loess lands much of the housing is in caves cut into the steep cliff sides. The loess is easily cut and provides warmth in winter and coolness in summer. It has one grave disadvantage; this is an unstable region, subject to earthquakes, which, when they occur, take a terrible toll of these cave dwellers.

In former generations the food of the *peh hsin*, the common people, has been monotonous and meagre, particularly during the lean winter months. The staple diet is boiled millet or kaoliang, *pao tzu* (steamed bread), *tu fu* (bean curd) and vegetables. Meat (pork and chicken) is eaten very sparingly, usually at feast times. Tea or boiled water is the universal drink. Chinese wine will appear only at feasts. This poor diet has been much improved of late due to increased production, better storage of grain and more equable distribution. The peasant of the north no longer lives so near the brink of subsistence.

Cotton, formerly dyed with native indigo, is the universal clothing. Padded clothes are essential in winter. Happily, nowadays, it is unusual to see anyone inadequately protected. The *pei wo* or padded cotton quilt serves for bedding and has the advantage of being easily carried when travelling.

Formerly, under-employment, due to the long winter period of enforced idleness, has been a big cause of poverty. The establishment of co-operatives and then communes has entirely changed this. Local factories, repair workshops and small chemical fertiliser works have absorbed many. Water conservancy works, road building and school building in the winter months have progressed to such an extent that there has been complaint of labour shortage. It is worth noting that in the past there has been a taboo in the north of women working in the fields except at certain times and seasons. This taboo has now gone and women are admitted to all kinds of work.

FISHERIES

The training grounds for sailors in all countries are the rugged coasts with their natural harbours and safe havens, eg the coast of Maine in USA and those of Cornwall and Devon in England. The south-east coast of China, stretching from Canton, Kwangtung to Ningpo, Chekiang, has just such a deeply indented ria coast with short, sharp rivers, narrow coastal plain and excellent harbours. It was mainly from here throughout history that China's overseas trade was carried on. The old port of Zayton was sited near to modern Amoy. It was from this coast that the tea clippers sailed in their races for Europe and USA in the later nineteenth century and it is from its many small harbours that most of China's sea fishing today is pursued. Shantung peninsula has a similar rugged coast. Fishing here has an additional hazard. Winter dust storms blowing from the land often amount to impenetrable fog.

Deep sea fishing is carred on in the Po-hai, Yellow and South China seas in big junks which are now almost universally mechanised. Their catch is chiefly large and small croaker and horsetail. A sailing junk can be converted for under 50,000 yuan (approximately £7,000) as compared with 560,000 yuan, the cost of building a 250hp trawler. Moreover, the converted vessel is better suited to the present technical level of fishermen's collective organisations. The junks themselves, for the most part, are the homes of the families of the crew. Ports are increasingly equipping themselves to deal with construction and the repair demands and with refrigeration plant. In-shore fishing has always been vigorously pursued and nearly everywhere the coastal waters have been over-fished. The catch includes cuttle-fish, prawns, sea-slugs, abalone, shellfish and seaweeds (*lami-naria*).

A very large amount of fish is caught and raised in the inland waters. The great rivers and lakes abound in fish, which are caught by net, cormorant and otter. Since Liberation there has been a great development of fish pond culture throughout the whole country. Even in Yunnan in 1965 had establishments in eighty-five counties. It is proving both productive and lucrative. In the south it is reckoned that one acre of fish pond is the equivalent of two acres of rice. The main types of fish raised are various kinds of carp, mandarin fish and anchovy. It is a common practice in the south to stock the flooded paddy field with fish after the rice has been planted out. The growing rice provides sufficient shade to protect the fish from the summer sun.

Fishermen, who were formerly notoriously exploited in marketing their catches, are now organised in co-operatives and communes and enjoy much greater social security.

FORESTRY

The main forested lands of China today lie in the Ta Ching Shan of the North-East and in the uplands of the western regions of the Yangtze and Si Kiang basins. The coniferous forests of the north are the country's main source of timber. While they are being heavily cut, they are, today, also being carefully conserved. Farther south the forests are composed of conifers and deciduous trees (Chinese fir, Japanese cedar, acacia, camphor) and, in the far south, tropical evergreens.

An appreciation of the value of tree cover has not been one of the outstanding characteristics of the Chinese peasant. In early centuries, as he moved southward into the densely forested lands of the Yangtze basin, trees were an enemy to be cleared for cultivation—an enemy all too thoroughly defeated. As population increased, first the valley bottoms, then the hillsides were cut to give way for crops. Great areas were shorn even of their grass cover as demand for fuel increased. The result has been widespread and serious gully erosion where the rains are heavy and wind erosion where they are light.

There was some rather academic consciousness of this danger in the early half of this century. Arbour Day was instituted and parties from schools would march out, seedlings in hand, to plant the hillsides. Little or no attention was given to the care of these seedlings and, if they survived natural hazards of weather and pest, their fate was sealed when the women went forth, sickle in hand, in search of winter fuel. It was not until after the People's Government came to power that the problem was seriously tackled. Real effort was put into educating the peasant to the importance of afforestation and its relation to his own well-being. Moreover, there was now a government whose writ ran and whose law was enforced.

Government plans in this sphere provide a good example of 'walking on two legs'. Each locality, each commune, is enjoined to look to the establishment of its own seed bed and the planting of its own hillsides. In addition the central government has set on foot grandiose schemes, the most spectacular of which is the establishment of a shelter belt of trees, 1,000 miles long and a mile wide, extending from north-east to south-west across the dry lands of the north. Quick-growing trees, such as fir, larch, poplar and birch are used. These efforts, not yet complete, have met with very considerable success.

5

How They Live and Work in the Cities

A PROBLEM which has puzzled more than one Westerner is why a country like China, with its early and profound knowledge of science, its genius for invention and its reputation for perseverance, should have been so late in the field of modern industrial development. For more than 2,000 years the Chinese have had a knowledge of polarity and in succeeding centuries have invented many ingenious machines, such as the astronomical clock, the water-powered blast furnace, the spinning wheel, the silk reeling machine and loom, the stern-post rudder, the deep drill. It seems strange that, until the twentieth century, this inventiveness remained dormant and China experienced no industrial revolution comparable with that of the West. The reason lies very largely in China's deeply rooted Confucian philosophy and the social pattern which resulted from it. The reader will remember the low esteem in which the merchant and entrepreneur were held by the gentry and scholar-administrator (Chapter 4, p 70). This does not mean that material things were despised but that their production, for the most part, was confined to handicraftsmanship. Nearly all industry was conducted under the guild system, consisting of small, independent masters, who had a few journeymen and apprentices in their employ. There was little division of labour; craftsmanship was of a high order; little or no machinery or power other than manpower was used; discipline was lax and easy; work was slow and often heavy. Even in highly developed

97

centres, such as the ceramics industry of Kingterchen, Kiangsi, this same guild organisation held. If production of any one commodity threatened to develop on a large scale, as for example salt, it was taken over as a state monopoly by the administration, almost inevitably succumbing to corruption. Satisfaction with the sufficiency of the economy was voiced in 1793 by Emperor Ch'ien Lung, who, in turning down Lord Macartney's mission to open trade between UK and China, said, 'Our Celestial Empire possesses all things in prolific abundance and lacks no product within its borders; there is, therefore, no need to import the manufactures of outside barbarians.'

This pattern of industrial organisation, or lack of it, continued well on into the nineteenth century. The first break came with the defeat of China in the wars of 1839–40 and 1857–60 and the opening of the treaty ports, permitting foreign merchants to enter and trade. There followed a considerable development of cottage industry and small workshop, working to the order of the merchant and entrepreneur, who began to intercept the normal direct contact between producer and consumer. But foreigners were primarily concerned with the collection of China's raw materials (tea, vegetable oils, cotton and other natural fibres) for export and with the building of railways, which would facilitate this collection and would service the mines which they were anxious to open. Because trade concessions had been forced at gunpoint and moreover the changes in themselves were anathema to the Court, the official attitude to this development was one of hostility and non-co-operation, at which none is more adept than the Chinese. In consequence foreign investment of capital tended to be confined to coastal and river ports and places not far inland, notably Shanghai and Tientsin, where it could be under gunboat protection.

The humiliating military defeats suffered by China led one or two governor-generals, notably Li Hung-chang and Chang Chih-tung, to attempt the modernisation of their forces by opening arsenals and shipyards. The latter built the Hanyang Iron Works, Wuhan, in 1896, primarily for making rails for the Peking–Hankow railway.

It was not until the treaty of Shimoseski, 1895, at the end of the Sino-Japanese war, that foreigners gained the right to engage in manufacturing in China. Thereafter there was a gradual development of joint stock companies but, even in 1933, it was estimated that there were only 250 factories which could be regarded as modern and that about three-quarters of production in China was handicraft. Chinese companies were at a disadvantage vis-à-vis foreigners in that the latter were exempt from *Likin*, a tax laid on transportation of goods within the country. This severely handicapped the Chinese merchant and added to the general resentment of the 'unequal treaties' and of Western imperialism. Unstable government, civil war and international war throughout the whole of the first half of the twentieth century militated against any steady or considerable industrial development. It was only after the peace and stability of the People's Government that real progress was possible.

By far the greatest modern industrial development was made in Manchuria. When Japan defeated Russia in 1904 she took over Russia's considerable influence in the North-East and set about developing the great natural resources of the area. This was further consolidated when, in 1931, Japan annexed Manchuria, created the state of Manchukuo and made the former Chinese emperor its nominal head. Anshan developed into a great integrated iron and steel centre and Shenyang (Mukden) into an engineering centre.

MINERAL RESOURCES

China is richly endowed with minerals, some of which have been worked from earliest times. The copper from which the early Shang bronzes were made may have been mined locally but the tin probably came from the south-west in Kweichow or Yunnan. Marco Polo (1254–1324) was clearly unacquainted with coal when he wrote, 'it is a fact that all over the country of Cathay there is a kind of black stone existing in beds in the mountains, which they dig out and burn like firewood.'

Coal

Coal deposits are enormous and widely dispersed, no province being without reasonable reserves. By far the greatest of these lie to the north of the Chinling axis. This northern area lay under shallow seas during Carboniferous and Permian times, during which huge beds of anthracite and bituminous coal were laid down. The richest fields lie in Shansi, Shensi and Honan. The North-East has considerable reserves of bituminous; its fields include the fantastic open-cast workings at Fushun and Fusin where seams vary between 100 and 300ft in thickness. Coal south of the Chinling axis is younger, mainly of Rhaetic origin since this part of the country was deeply submerged in Carboniferous times. The main fields here are in the south-west (Szechwan, Yunnan and Kweichow). The least favoured provinces are those of the south-east (Kiangsu, Fukien, Chekiang). Large fields of bituminous coal exist in Sinkiang to the north of Tien Shan; since 1949 large deposits have been found in the Tsaidam. There is comparatively little lignite in China, the two main fields being in Heilungkiang and Shansi.

Total coal reserves in 1934 were estimated to be about 280,000 million tons. Although extensive surveys have been carried out by the People's Government, no comparable figure has been published beyond that in *Ten Great Years* (Peking, 1959), which gave proved reserves as 80,000 million tons with the note, 'These reserves can be used as a basis for designing capital construction and investment'. Some idea of the growth of coal production during the twentieth century can be gained from the following figures:

Year	Tons	
1912	13,000,000	
1930	16,000,000	half in Manchuria
1944	71,263,000	(under Japanese)
1945	32,430,000	
1958	270,000,000	
1967	190,000,000	(foreign estimate)

Since Liberation, production methods have been continuously modernised and mechanised. Safety measures, which were conspicuous by their absence before 1949, are now reasonably enforced and precautions against miners' diseases, such as silicosis, are taken.

Iron ore

While it was realised that there was ample coal to meet the needs of modern industry, experts were agreed that the lack of iron ore of high enough content would effectively prevent China from ever becoming a highly industrialised nation. Her leading geologist, Dr J. S. Lee, stated in 1939, 'It is quite clear that China can never become an iron producing country of any importance.' With the exception of Liaoning in the North-East (Manchuria), which was under Japanese control, there were few places known to have high grade iron ore. One such area was at Tayeh, Hupeh, which was estimated to contain nearly 150 million tons of ore whose iron content was 56–60 per cent. It was on this ore that the Hanyang Iron Works, mentioned above, were based. Unfortunately for China, both the Iron Works and the Tayeh iron ore came under Japanese control before World War I and remained so until 1945, the iron ore being shipped to Japan for smelting. During World War II Japan exploited Liaoning iron ore to the full and in 1943 produced, 1,726,000 tons of pig iron and 837,000 tons of steel.

On attaining power in 1949 the Communists set on foot a most vigorous and comprehensive survey of the country's mineral wealth. Survey teams discovered that iron ore is present in far greater quantity and quality than previously supposed. Moreover, modern smelting techniques have made the use of low content ores economically viable.

Oil

The presence of oil and natural gas in Szechwan was known in later Han times at the beginning of the Christian era. Its

use was confined to the refining of salt in the province and no
further development occurred.

At the beginning of the twentieth century large quantities of
kerosene were being imported through American, Dutch and
British oil companies—'oil for the lamps of China'—the small
paraffin lamp being in universal use wherever the trader could
penetrate. Any suggestion that there were local oilfields which
could be exploited was strongly discounted either from a
genuine belief that China's geological structure precluded the
possibility or from a desire to preserve a highly profitable
market.

After 1949 prospecting teams quickly discovered rich oilfields, which, during the succeeding twenty years, have been
opened up so that today China can supply all her rapidly
growing needs. It is estimated that over 8 million tons were
produced in 1963. Exclusive of the oil produced from oil shale,
there are five main fields; the Karamai field in Dzungaria was
opened between 1953 and 1957 with the help of Russian sur-
veyors and technicians. It is now entirely under Chinese direction. Production rose rapidly and now approaches 2 million
tons a year. Karamai is connected by pipeline to Tushantzu,
where there is a refinery. Two other fields in the dry north-

---

An acrobatic performance by members of the People's Liberation Army in a Peking park on 1 October 1971. Such shows,
though usually on a smaller scale, are a common and
popular form of amusement.

A woman doctor of the PLA leading a medical team in Hainan
among the poor and lower-middle peasants of the Li and
Miao people. The army medical service does a considerable
amount of work among the civil population.

毛主席万岁
把医疗卫生
工作的重点放
到农村去

west have been found and developed since 1949, one in the Yumen area and the other in the Tsaidam. Both are productive and have their own refineries. Modern development of the Szechwan field proved disappointing until the discovery of new deposits in 1958. The most recent (1965) discovery and the one which has received most publicity is the Taching field in north Heilungkiang in the Tsitsihar area. It is publicised so widely not only because of the productivity it promises but also for the spirit of unselfishness 'for the masses' which, it is claimed, has been so strongly evinced in the development of the field in the very severe bitter conditions of the north. Oil from oil shale is produced mainly in the North-East at Fushun, Hwalien and Mutankiang. The most notable of these is at Fushun where a stratum of oil shale, 300ft thick, lies above the open-cast coal measures. This shale was first exploited by the Japanese and was (and still is) refined on the site. A recent and important development of oil shale is at Mowming in the south-west corner of Kwangtung.

Non-ferrous minerals

Although, for long, China has been known to be rich in non-

A 'barefoot doctor' giving acupuncture treatment to a patient in Yunnan. Acupuncture, accepted and accredited in old China, is now being widely practised and is used in major surgery in China.

A batch of *Kaifang* (Liberation) lorries ready for despatch from Changchun (Kirin) No 1 Motor Vehicle Plant. Other big motor producing centres are Loyang, Tientsin, Shenyang, Tsinan and Wuhan.

ferrous metals, few have been exploited to any extent until recently. Even copper, which was required for the bronze vessels of the Shang and Chou dynasties and for copper coinage throughout the succeeding centuries, was never heavily mined. The highest recorded production of copper was 1,600 tons in 1727.

Surveys carried out since Liberation have revealed that China's reserves in tin, tungsten, manganese, antimony and molybdenum are among the richest in the world. The oldest, best surveyed and richest areas, according to present knowledge, are the provinces south of the Yangtze. South Hunan, South Kiangsi and North Kwangtung are particularly rich in tungsten (wolfram). Extensive finds of all these have been made during the last decade in the North-East. Further discoveries of copper, manganese and salt have been made in the upper Hwang-ho region and in Chinghai. All these minerals have been developed vigorously since 1949. Output is being absorbed almost entirely in indigenous manufacture. China's production of 42,000 tons of antimony led the world in 1916. It is used in the manufacture of pewter, white metal, and printer's type. Its main centre of production is Hunan and it is processed in Wuhan. Production virtually ceased during the civil war and Sino-Japanese war but good recovery has been made since 1949 and it is again a valuable export.

Development of industry since Liberation

We have seen that during the first half of the twentieth century the bulk of foreign capital was invested near the littoral, where it was more easily under the protection of foreign gunboats. Chinese capital tended to gather under this umbrella with the result that such modern industrial development as took place was largely confined to the coastal areas. Even before 1949 it had been Communist declared policy to reverse this concentration and to achieve a wide dispersal of industry. There were three main objectives behind this policy. The first was strategic—ensuring the safety of vital industrial centres from foreign attack. No one living in China in 1950 during the Korean war, when General MacArthur's forces were approaching the Yalu River and threatening the industrial complex of the North-East (Shenyang, Anshan, Fushun), could have failed to sense the widespread alarm throughout China. There was a determination that this danger should not occur again. During the succeeding twenty years integrated iron and steel works have been established in practically every province. The second objective in dispersing industry was an economic one. In view of widespread natural economic wealth, it was clear that a vast amount of transportation costs could be saved by the establishment of local centres, which would, moreover, create local markets and demand. The third reason for dispersal was psychological. The coastal development of industry, largely under foreign direction, was a constant reminder of Western imperialism and was an offence to national dignity and pride. In those early days of Liberation it had to be expunged; probably today this need is largely forgotten.

Iron and steel

On the defeat of Japan in 1945, Russian troops moved in and occupied the North-East in accordance with the Yalta agreement. When they withdrew, they virtually stripped the region of its Japanese heavy industrial equipment, thus stagnating production. After Liberation, modern, fully automated and integrated iron and steel plant from USSR was installed at Anshan. This turns out a full range of heavy steel products. These enormous works stand comparison with the biggest complexes in Europe and USA. Following the re-establishment of heavy industry in the North-East, two other large integrated works were built at Wuhan and Paotow. That at Wuhan revived, although not on the same site, the former Hanyang Iron Works, built in 1897. Since then further works have been opened all over the country, most notable of which are in Chungking, Taiyuan, Kunming, Maanshan and Kiuchuan (Suchow). Continuing geological surveys have shown that there is adequate iron ore to meet the needs of this rapidly growing industry. The discovery of rich deposits at Chingtiehshan, Kansu, have been responsible for very rapid development of the iron and steel industry in the north-west.

Pre-Liberation production reached a peak in 1943 when the Japanese were pressing output from the North-East to meet their war needs. 1,883,000 tons of pig iron, 923,000 tons of ingot steel and 486,000 tons of finished steel were then produced. At that time 65 per cent of China's total ingot steel production was in Japanese hands. Output in 1949 was down nearly to zero; by 1952 production had so far recovered that it was near to the previous peak. The last firm figures are those for 1959: pig iron 9,500,000 tons, ingot steel 8,630,000, finished steel 9,200,000. The most reliable estimates of present production of ingot steel give figures between 8 to 10,000,000 tons. Not only has China greatly increased its output but, probably equally important, it claims now to be producing every kind and quality of steel needed for modern industry.

ENGINEERING AND MACHINERY

One of the most urgent needs, if industrialisation were to be achieved, has been the production of tools and tool making equipment. Both Shenyang and Shanghai were engaged in this work before 1949 but since then their plant has been greatly expanded. Both centres have concentrated largely on the construction of complete installations—blast furnaces, rolling mills, mining equipment, hydro-electric plant etc. The Shenyang Heavy Machinery Plant specialises in making lathes of all kinds and sizes and turbine motors. Shanghai is proud of having produced a 12,000 ton hydraulic free-forging press, done largely without the aid of the sophisticated machinery commonly used in the West. In addition to these two established centres, the country now abounds in engineering plants. Many cities are already noted for their specialised products: for example Loyang for ball bearings, Urumchi for agricultural machinery,

Wuhan for machine tools and agricultural pumps, Nanning for rice transplanters, Tatung for locomotives. Great progress has been made in recent years in the development of high precision machinery. There are few, if any, of the most delicate machines and instruments that cannot be made in China today. Peking, Tientsin, Nanking, Shanghai and Shenyang are the outstanding centres for this work.

CHEMICALS

China's chemical industry was virtually non-existent in 1949 in spite of its large natural resources. The imperative demand for rapid and continuous increase in agricultural production has naturally led to concentration on development of chemical fertiliser, especially since the lean years of 1960–1. Emphasis has been laid on widespread production in small- and medium-sized plant, utilising local resources and also avoiding excessive transport costs. Whereas in the pre-Liberation period output was confined to ammonium sulphate, today's production covers the whole field of fertilisers.

Chinese chemists claim that they are now producing the whole range of pharmaceutical and plastic products and, by their own researches, discovering new medicines. The main chemical centres at present are Shanghai, Tientsin, Taiyuan, Lanchow and Kirin. New and large development may soon be expected at Sinning, based on the great salt field in the Tsaidam.

The following index figures give some indication of the growth of the industry, using the pre-Liberation peak year as 100:

	1949	*1952*	*1958*
Sulphuric acid	22·2	105·6	411·1
Soda ash	85·4	186·4	621·4
Caustic soda	125·0	658·3	2,250·0
Chemical fertiliser	11·9	79·7	357·3

MOTOR VEHICLES

The Chinese motor industry is exclusively a child of the People's Republic. All motor vehicles before 1949 were imported, mainly from USA. As might be expected, production has a marked utilitarian flavour, being concentrated almost exclusively on trucks (lorries), public transport buses, coaches and tractors of all sizes and power. Only in recent years have limousines been manufactured; they are largely reserved for the use of government officials and the entertainment of foreign guests. The first large motor works were built in Loyang, Honan, which specialises in heavy tractors and bulldozers; Tientsin in the 'Iron Ox' 45hp tractor, trucks and coaches; Anshan in the 100hp 'Red Flag' tractor; Wuhan in the 7hp walking tractor and so on. Today more than a dozen cities are heavily engaged in motor manufacture.

TEXTILES

Until towards the close of the nineteenth century the clothing of the common people of China was made chiefly from hemp and ramie. Cotton was a luxury. Today it is the universal clothing material in China Proper. The growth of cotton has risen by leaps and bounds and has been extended by irrigation into the dry north-west. *Ten Great Years* states that in 1949 China's output was 8,890,000 tan (1 tan = 133lb) as compared with USA's 70,150,000 tan. In 1958 the figures were 42,000,000 and 50,420,000 respectively. Shanghai, Wuhan and Tientsin are still the most important cotton manufacturing towns but new centres are being opened annually, notably at Lanchow in the newly developed Kansu cotton fields and at Sian in the Wei valley. In spite of this big increase, supply has not yet caught up with demand and cotton cloth is still rationed.

Silk, the oldest and most romantic textile, has always been

the luxury clothing of the rich. Its production, centred mainly in the lower Yangtze valley, declined seriously in the first half of the twentieth century. Helped by better sericulture and manufacturing methods it is recovering rapidly and is proving a useful booster to China's foreign trade balance. Woollen clothing is becoming increasingly popular in the north. Improved supplies of raw wool from the grasslands of the northwest are serving the many new mills that have opened in that region.

BUILDING INDUSTRY AND CEMENT

Perhaps most spectacular of all advances in modernisation under the People's Republic has been the amount of all kinds of building that has been achieved in twenty years. The writer, returning to Wuchang in 1956 after an absence of only five years, was quite lost in the development that had taken place to the east of the city. Public buildings, sports arenas, colleges and technical institutions are usually built of reinforced concrete. Dwellings, workers' flats and many industrial buildings are mostly of grey brick, often giving them a rather dull, dreary appearance. The urgency of demand has dictated that economy and utility shall be the rule. Happily, pressure on land has not been as keen as in USA and UK so that, except in the heart of such cities as Shanghai, skyscrapers are the exception rather than the rule. Blocks of workers' flats are rarely more than three of four storeys high.

The demand for buildings, roads, dams and bridges has led to a great development of cement works in all parts of the country where the raw materials are available. Before Liberation only two large works were in existence, one in Tongshan, Hopei, and the other at Shihhweiyao, Hupeh, the latter opened only in 1948. Since then at least 12 large and 100 small works have been built.

LIGHT INDUSTRIES

A vast number of manufactures have come under the direction of the Ministry of Light Industry.

China's once world renowned ceramics industry fell to a very low ebb during the unrest in the first half of this century. Since 1949 there has been a steady flow in the tide of rehabilitation. The former famous kilns at Liling (near Pingsiang, Hunan) and King-teh-chen (Kiangsi) are again in full production, turning out high grade under-glazed porcelain ware. Fahshan is producing porcelain figurines; Chekiang, green ware; Honan, *chun* porcelain. All of these are finding increasing indigenous and foreign markets. Main production, however, is concentrated on turning out large quantities of good, attractive china ware for the masses in place of the coarse pottery in former general use. King-teh-chen kilns alone produced 85 million pieces in 1965. Many new sites are being developed, such as that at Shihtsuishan, Ningsia, which was opened in 1951 and is producing fine porcelain. Transportation is mainly by river and canal.

Food products, processing and canning have quickly assumed vast proportions. They range throughout the land from meat canning and dairy products in Inner Mongolia to fruit canning, notably pineapple in Hainan. Soaps and detergents, paper making, salt refining all fall within the Ministry's ambit, as also do many light manufactures. Bicycles are now produced in large numbers; also shoes, mainly rubber or plastic soled, plastic products of all kinds, electric torches, vacuum flasks and so on. All of these were formerly beyond the means of the masses but now find a ready market.

HANDICRAFTS

In former centuries nearly all China's production of material things was done by craftsmen. Usually one family or household specialised in one particular branch of a craft, eg making guest-room furniture or painting freehand the decorations on that furniture. As we have seen, each craft had its guild. Great skill and dexterity were developed and, with them, independence and individualism. Regions became renowned for their specialities: eg Swatow for drawn thread embroidery; Changsha for bamboo work.

In spite of the great development in modern industry in the last two decades, a large amount of work is still done by these families of craftsmen. The government has been very conscious of the need to handle these individualistic workers with care as it tries to convert them from a capitalistic to a communistic outlook. T'ien Ping, writing in the Peking *Ta-hung Pao* (*People's Daily*) in 1964, said:

> *It is necessary to adopt methods of persuasion, of giving example and of offering them state assistance, so that they will consciously and voluntarily get organised and take the road to co-operation . . . Handicraft workers in our country have rich experience in production. They are nimble-minded and clever and dexterous in using their hands, and are resourceful and full of inventive spirit . . . Since the handicraft industry deals mostly with small products, the scale of the enterprise should not be too large and the degree of centralisation should not be too high. Attention should therefore be paid to preserving its small and flexible features.*

Today the overwhelming majority of handicraftsmen are organised in handicraft co-operatives and co-operative factories. Production is said to have increased greatly and quality to have improved. Soochow, one of the great art handicraft regions, opened an art handicraft centre in 1958 on a part-work, part-study basis and has trained well over 1,000 apprentices in designing, modelling, decoration, restoration and retouching old paintings.

URBAN COMMUNES

While the rural commune embraces a considerable area, the urban commune is, by definition, a much more compact community. There is a general pattern or theme to which all urban communes conform but, as in the rural communes, there is an almost infinite variety within the pattern. They are organised on a basis of streets or lanes within a defined ward or precinct and may include as many as 10,000 to 12,000 families, say 60,000 people. These elect their Resident Committee, who are responsible for most of the activities within their area, including law and order, industrial production, retail shops, public health, street cleanliness, education and social activities.

Perhaps the most striking achievement of the urban commune has been in housing. In many cities slum clearance has been tackled energetically. Old buildings have been renovated or rebuilt, though maybe not to standards acceptable to the West. New three or four storeyed concrete or brick-built flats for workers have sprung up everywhere, a flat usually giving accommodation of a living-room of about 12ft × 10ft, a kitchen, a toilet with running water and perhaps a balcony. Rents are low, varying between 5 and 20 yuan a month according to the accommodation offered. Roads have been remade and public drainage installed. A new standard of street cleanliness has arisen, maintained largely by the old people, students and soldiers, which puts that of most European and American cities to shame.

The staple food eaten will naturally vary with the region: wheat and 'mant'ou' (steamed bread) in the north and rice in the south. Since factories, workshops, schools and dwellings are much more closely gathered than in rural communes, many more meals are taken in institutional canteens. A usual practice is for husband, wife and children to take their midday meal at their respective canteens and for the family to gather at home for the evening meal. A close eye is always kept on the relative costs.

In the field of health the urban commune has a clear advantage over the rural. Whereas the latter has to rely on the 'barefoot' doctor and clinic, the former usually has the city hospital services, which are steadily rising in standard. In addition to Western medicine and surgery, traditional Chinese medicine and, in particular, acupuncture (needling) are offered to patients. Acupuncture is now being used successfully as an anaesthetic in major surgery.

Reliance on mutual help in the care of the old, lonely and sick is all part of the new morality. Old people are still cared for generally by the younger generations of their own families but more and more homes for old people are being built, especially in the highly industrialised areas. For example, retired miners in Fushan without family have a comfortable home and club in which to pass their declining years. Urban communes everywhere have crèches and nursery schools at which working mothers can leave their offspring. Here again a sharp eye will be kept on the balance between the cost of crèche and take-home pay of the mother.

The success of urban communes has varied greatly from region to region and even within individual cities. Their industrial output in 1959 and 1960 undoubtedly was considerable but, after the lean years of 1961–2, the call on 'industry to serve agriculture' and the return to the countryside, there was a marked decline in the importance of the urban communes.

URBAN WORKER

An essential difference between the rural and urban worker is the basis of remuneration. The former, as we have seen, is paid by work points and receives his pay partly in kind. The latter is on a wage basis. Government policy has consistently been to keep wages low, to maintain a wage ceiling of approximately 200 yuan (£30 or $75) a month, to 'cut down the "tall poppies" ', ie to eliminate high incomes but to have some differential within low limits. Workers are accordingly graded. The following figures, which vary from region to region, give a rough approximation of monthly rates: apprentices 25–40 yuan; workers (8 grades) 40–110 yuan; technicians (5 grades) 50–100 yuan; managers 70–160 yuan according to the size of the concern and responsibility; engineers (9 grades) 90–200 yuan.

A manager of a medium-sized enterprise, earning 140 yuan a month, and his wife, a teacher, earning 60 yuan a month, having one child of nursery school age, might budget their expenditure for the month as follows:

Midday meals at canteen and school	65 yuan
Home meals	55 yuan
Clothes, entertainment, books etc	25 yuan
Rent	15 yuan
Nursery school	15 yuan
Savings	25 yuan
	200 yuan

Clothes are cheap and are made to last. A summer cotton suit for man or woman would cost about 10 yuan and a winter padded one nearly double. Savings might be for things such as a bicycle, radio or watch, any of which would cost between 100 and 150 yuan.

For some years after Liberation there was contention between payment by time and piece rates. The contradiction was largely resolved during the Great Cultural Revolution in favour of time rates as being more in line with Mao Tse-tung's thought. Piece rates came under heavy criticism as encouraging the 'economism' of Liu Shao-ch'i. There are also other weighty reasons why time rates are more fitting in China today. The satisfactory functioning of piece rates demands thorough, highly sophisticated costing and trained management, conditions which are not easily met at present.

TRADE UNIONS

The first Trade Unions in China were formed in 1920. Their purpose was quite simply the protection of the worker against exploitation by employer; their progress was turbulent. In 1948 the All China Trade Union Federation was formed and remained in existence until it was dissolved at the outbreak of the Cultural Revolution in 1966.

Trade Unions under the People's Government are regarded in a quite different light from those in the capitalist world of the West. In the West they are bodies representing the interests of the workers largely in contention with the employers. In China the Trade Unions are an integral part of the socialist system and, while their function is the promotion of the workers' cultural and material welfare, the basis is essentially one of co-operation. The Constitution specifically states that the unions are there 'to play the part of a strong assistant to the Party'. Membership is confined to industrial workers, agriculturalists having their own organisation, and is compulsory. Numbers have grown from under 3 million members in 1949 to 40 million in 1960. Trade Union elections follow the same pattern as those of State elections.

Broadly speaking the unions have two main functions. On the one hand they are charged above all else with securing political correctness in the workers and in maintaining their enthusiasm, thus stimulating production and implementing the slogan 'compare with others, emulate the advanced and help the backward'. On the other hand they are a very important part of the country's educational and social organisation. Their duties include a regard for the safety of working conditions, factory canteens, workers' clubs and rest houses, workers' recreation, people's palaces, games stadia and the like, factory schools, libraries (of which, it is reported, there are over 30,000), and technical colleges. The educational activities of the unions have been largely instrumental in reducing illiteracy from an estimated 85 per cent in 1949 to 15 per cent in 1961.

During the early years after Liberation, Trade Unions had little to do with the fixing of wages, but more recently they have been drawn into the work of fixing wage scales and work norms. They claim that largely through their work real wages have risen 100 per cent. The right to strike is secured in the Constitution but it has seldom been resorted to, and then only at local level over such issues as working conditions. The very close liaison between worker and management largely avoids the contentions met with in USA and Europe. Edgar Snow in *Red China Today* quotes Li Chi-po, Vice-Chairman of All-China Trade Union Federation, as saying, 'Labour unions cannot fight for the narrow interests of any particular craft union at the expense of the whole people.' The road to higher wages is either through the orthodox channels when rates are fixed annually for the whole concern or through the individual worker qualifying for a higher grade.

Trade Unions obtain their funds through levies of 1 per cent of the member's wage and 2 per cent from the wages bill of the enterprise, together with any profits coming from canteen catering, sale of publications etc.

FOREIGN TRADE

China has never evinced great interest in trade outside its borders. True, there was trade in silk and glass between Rome and China in Han times and some development of overseas trade by Arab sailors between China, Japan and Korea in the T'ang dynasty. But it was not until the Treaty Ports were opened in the mid nineteenth century that foreign trade assumed any large proportions.

In the 1920s Hong Kong, Japan, USA and UK were China's main customers. Hong Kong was the great entrepôt through which more than one-quarter of foreign trade passed. At that time China's main exports were raw silk and silk piece goods, soyabeans, tea, skins and hides, peanuts and wood-oil. Her imports were cotton goods, rice from Indo-China, kerosene, sugar, raw cotton, cigarettes and machinery. This general shape of trade continued until the revolution of 1949 when big changes took place.

The greatest of these changes was the transference of all foreign trade from private hands to governmental control. All trade with the outside world is now in the hands of the Ministry of Foreign Trade. The actual work is conducted by fourteen large corporations which have trade centres in all Communist and some non-Communist countries, eg Hong Kong, London and Berne. A glance at China's export figures below will show how important a part Hong Kong plays in securing for China a favourable trade balance.

USA, so important a trader before 1949, laid a tight embargo on all commerce with China during the Korean war in 1950. Only in recent years has this embargo been slightly relaxed; President Nixon's visit to China in 1972 brought some hope of a real renewal of trade between the two countries.

The following figures (in million US $) give some idea of the flow of trade:

	Imports	
	1960	*1965*
USSR	817	189
Cuba	60 (estimated)	97
Japan	27	245
Australia	23	167 (wheat)
Canada	9	97 (wheat)
West Germany	5	79
UK	89	72
Hong Kong	21	13

	Exports	
USSR	848	225
Cuba	—	129
Hong Kong	207	406
Japan	21	225
West Germany	69	73
UK	70	83

The disastrous harvests of 1960–1 account for the heavy imports of wheat from Australia and Canada in the succeeding years. These were paid for in cash and imports have now ceased. China's exports still consist largely of agricultural raw materials and her imports of machinery and industrial raw materials. This imbalance is steadily being redressed as her industrial development progresses.

THE FAMILY AND THE STATUS OF WOMEN

One of the highest virtues in ancient China was the maintenance of continuity of the family through male issue. Confucian ethics laid down the standards of loyalty, kinship, ritual and behaviour which bound the old extended family into a close, inward looking and intensely clannish group. However, it was only the wealthier classes who were able to maintain this extended family organisation and were able to enjoy the corporate security it provided. Generally speaking the lower down the scale of affluence the smaller the family group became and with it greater loss of security.

The position of women under this old family system was unenviable. It is revealing to note that in the *lo ch'in* or six family relationships (husband and wife, parents and child, brother and brother) no reference is made to sisters. Girls had no place or significance in this respect. They served their parents until marriage, in which they had no say. Thereafter the married girl served in her husband's family under the authority of the grandmother, the *t'ai t'ai*, a rule which could be benevolent but, far more generally, is reported to have been harsh and autocratic in the extreme, leading at times to suicide. On the other hand spinstership was a state to be avoided almost at all costs. Hence the institution of arranged marriages, concubinage and poligamy, which left women virtually without rights.

Victor Purcell, in his *China*, maintains with considerable justification that the greatest achievement of the Communist revolution has been the emancipation of women. Many of women's disabilities were made illegal under Kuomingtang law but the law remained largely inoperative. It was not until the People's Government passed the Marriage Law (Document 33) and implemented it that women achieved real emancipation.

Today arranged marriages and polygamy are illegal, although a fair amount of mild arrangement and go-between probably still takes place, particularly in rural areas. Prostitution and concubinage, which under the old system were rampant, largely as compensation for lack of romance under arranged marriages, are forbidden. Divorce, at the demand of either party, is obtainable but care is taken to maintain the partnership if possible; the rights and care of any children by the marriage are specially safeguarded.

Women have equal rights with men to all kinds of work, equal pay for equal work and the right to hold property, which formerly was almost unknown. Since 1949 women have qualified for and entered into all kinds of work with great enthusiasm, including not only all the professions but also heavy industry and engineering. Their freedom in all these fields contrasts strangely with John Foster Dulles's wild statement that 'the individual is valued and allowed to survive only as a labourer of the state. "All-purpose" workers, in blocs of tens of thousands, are herded in crude dormitories, with men and children largely segregated and the children placed in wholesale nurseries so that women can also be put to slave labour.'

6

How They Learn

THERE have been at least eleven major peasant revolts in Chinese history, each having as its object the overthrow of effete and corrupt emperors, who, by their dissolute lives and oppressive government, have forfeited the 'mandate of heaven' to rule their people. Even when these revolutions have been successful and the dynasty overthrown the peasantry have quickly found themselves no better off, for the administrative skills and governmental 'know how' lay in the hands of the gentry, who were the only educated class. No matter how successful the fighting men might be the scholar-administrator class was quickly back in the governmental saddle directing affairs. Mao Tse-tung is very conscious of this repetition of history; he goes to great lengths to defeat a further recurrence.

THE OLD EDUCATIONAL SYSTEM

As far back in Chinese history as the later part of the Chou dynasty (1122–255 BC) in the days of Lao Tzu and Confucius, entry into official employment required a thorough knowledge of the Six Virtues (wisdom, benevolence, goodness, righteousness, loyalty and harmony) and the Six Arts (ritual, music, archery, charioteering, writing and mathematics), the object of which was to promote the *Chuin tzu*, the upright, princely man to whom alone government could be safely confided. It was not long before these requirements were formalised and an examination system for candidates was instituted in the Han dynasty

(202 BC–AD 220). There were three grades of scholarship: the *Hsiu-ts'ai* (BA), in which the successful candidate was re-examined every three years; the *Chu-jen* (MA); and the *Chin-shih* (DLitt). The latter could then graduate into *Han Lin*, the Imperial Academy. Success in these examinations entailed an enormous amount of learning by rote. Not only had the scholar to know and write many thousands of characters but he also had to commit a great deal of the classics and the commentaries on them to memory. This ability to memorise has become habitual and has spilled down to the present day, as the writer well remembers. A careless setting of a middle school examination question in 1924 revealed the fact that a large proportion of the class knew the textbook by heart and could quote any part of it at will.

The old system was élitist in the extreme and was virtually the preserve of the gentry, who alone had time and means to undertake the onerous study. Examinations were theoretically open to all and it was always the hope and ambition of families of the lower orders that one of its members would rise to the scholars' ranks. The rest of the family would save and scrape and live in poverty to enable a chosen boy to get the necessary teaching, but 'strait was the gate and narrow the way' and very few found it.

INTRODUCTION OF WESTERN LEARNING

It was into this educational set-up that modern Western education made its debut in the 1860s. Following the 'Lorcha' war of 1857 and the signing of the Treaty of Tientsin in 1860, missionary activity was permitted throughout the country. Unlike the Jesuits of the seventeenth and eighteenth centuries, whose contacts had been essentially with the Chinese literati, the missionaries of the nineteenth century, both Protestant and Roman Catholic, were evangelical and directed their attention to the *pai hsing*, the common people. In order to further their preaching the Bible was translated into *pai hua*, ie colloquial speech. It was received with utter scorn by Chinese scholars as a prostitution of the written word, dedicated as they were to *wen li*, the established literary form. None the less *pai hua* has had a profound influence since today it forms the basis of *p'u t'ung hua*, 'usual words' now in universal use throughout the land. Schools and hospitals quickly followed in the wake of the evangelists and their churches. Britain and particularly USA poured in vast quantities of money in building hundreds of primary and secondary (middle) schools. Protestant missions united in establishing colleges and universities in many provinces, most noted being Yen Ching University (now Peking University) and PUMC (Peking Union Medical College). Because USA played so large a part in this movement, education inevitably took on a predominantly American pattern, adopting largely its terminology, its curriculum and its credit system. This pattern was followed also by provincial governments after the formation of the Republic in 1911 as they slowly developed their own educational systems. It was largely through the intense interest in this educational field that USA developed, in the first half of the twentieth century, a paternalistic attitude to China, regarding itself as mentor, guiding the young Republic into the ways of the democratic West. It therefore came as a severe blow when this role was summarily and emphatically rejected in 1949.

Thus it was that Christian missions pioneered the road to universal education in China. High regard for learning was evinced by the eagerness with which the common people strove to secure a place in school for at least one of the family. School attendance was a privilege keenly sought. Primary schools were co-educational and were an early thin end of the wedge of women's emancipation. Boys in the family gained priority in attendance at middle schools but girls came more into their own as missions opened schools for them. Capacity for perseverance, hard work and 'stickability' are Chinese characteristics, which are no less evident in scholastic work than in other fields. More often than not it is necessary to urge restraint on a pupil rather than to goad. The writer looks back to days in 1924 when, as a young teacher in a middle school, he was required to make midnight tours of the dormitories to prevent boys working by candlelight under their blanket-draped beds, such was their keenness to learn.

In spite of the efforts made by the young Ministry of Education formed in 1920 and the efforts of Christian missions, education touched only a fringe of the problem. In 1920 it was estimated that there were only 6 million children in primary schools in the whole of China; in 1928 only 8 million. Intense anti-foreign, anti-imperialist feeling aroused during the Northern Expedition in 1926–7 led to the closing of all mission schools. They were re-opened under Chinese leadership in 1928 and continued to function until 1949, when all education came under government control. The years between 1928 and 1934 were hopeful ones in the educational field but growing civil war between Nationalist and Communist and then the Japanese invasion in 1937 brought disruption, many schools and universities in east and central China trekking 1,000 miles west into the mountains of Kweichow and Yunnan, returning only in 1946.

THE NEW APPROACH

The ancient educational system had as its aim the creation of an élite class of upright, princely men, who, by their correct behaviour, their good and just government and their wisdom, would so set an example that the common people would learn by it and follow it happily and contentedly. The modern Western attitude to learning leans rather to the pursuit of knowledge and the training of the mind than to the creation of a particular type and outlook. Perhaps the closest parallel to the old Chinese objective of producing men of a definite character is to be found in the British public school system, which certainly used to produce men of a clearly discernible type.

Both the old Confucian and the Western approaches were anathema to the CCP. In their eyes the former was feudal and fostered deeply those class distinctions which the Party is pledged to destroy. As has been mentioned, the scholar-administrator class had proved in history its resilience and its ability time and again to return to power; therefore it was doubly suspect in Communist eyes. The indignities and even persecution to which the literati have been subjected at times during the last twenty years are evidence of the watch that is kept to see that they do not achieve undue influence.

However, in spite of their radically opposed approaches, the Confucian and the Communist have one thing in common: both set out to effect a moral change in man. The Communist aim is nothing less than to effect a radical change in men's minds from self-seeking and regarding life in terms of use to self to thinking in terms of unselfishness and of service of the people. The prime purpose of education is to assist in this change. When Mao Tse-tung talks of political correctness being of first importance it is of this moral change he is speaking. In his work *On the Correct Handling of Contradictions among the People* he says, 'Our educational policy must enable everyone who receives an education to develop morally, intellectually and physically and become a worker with both socialist consciousness and culture.' All teaching in no matter what field or subject must have this end in view. Lecturers and teachers in China will remember how they were required, in the heady days of 1949 and 1950, to ask themselves what was the purpose or objective of each session before embarking on it, an embarrassing but salutary question for those who are in a rut.

Western education is equally—or even more—suspect in Communist eyes, not so much on account of the subject matter taught, much of which is common to East and West, but because, it is contended, it is the child and handmaid of capitalism and imperialism and fosters the very class distinctions which Communism is out to destroy.

FULL-TIME EDUCATION

In 1949 the People's Government took over an educational system based mainly on US practice, organised on the usual pattern of upper and lower primary school, junior and senior high (middle or secondary) school and university. This pattern remained in operation with no drastic change until GPCR (1966). Primary school covered six years' schooling, ages 8–10 in lower and 11–13 in upper, remembering that the Chinese reckon a child as one year old at birth. High school also covered six years and was divided into Junior 14–16 and Senior 17–19. To these, crèches and kindergartens were added very soon after 1949, catering for children of 3–7 years. These were and still are very varied in character. They are mainly day schools; some cater for weekly boarders; some are of a very temporary character, being 'ad hoc' institutions formed to help out parents during seasonal occurrences such as harvesting. It is estimated that there were about 120 million pupils in primary and 90 million in high school in 1965 and that some extra 40 million and 30 million places respectively would be required in the next 20 years.

Government policy has been to achieve universal compulsory education as quickly as possible. This has called for a tremendous amount of building during the past twenty years. Schools for the most part are plain and functional and have been built by the local communes in response to the call for 'self-reliance'. In consequence there is generally considerable local pride in achievement and interest in the school's activities. School equipment is generally minimal but will vary to some extent with the wealth of the local community. Kindergartens are provided with appropriate-sized chairs and desks and usually have gaily decorated enamel wash bowls.

The school year is divided into two terms, running from September to January and from March to July. Until 1966 it consisted of a total of 34 weeks and each week of six working days of six hours. The winter school holiday falls at Chinese New Year (January–February) and the summer holiday in August. China faces the same problems of getting to and from school as were faced in UK and USA at the turn of the century, when there were no cars and buses. Many children in outlying hamlets have to walk long distances daily.

Schools before the GPCR were run by a committee consisting of headmaster or headmistress, deputy head and representatives from the assistant teachers, who in turn reported to the full staff and parents' committee. The curriculum and timetable are laid down by the Minister of Education. In primary schools nearly half the time, ie 12 hours a week during the six years, has to be spent on language, such is the burden of learning Chinese characters. A further six hours a week is devoted to arithmetic, when calculating with the abacus or *suan p'an* is learnt. On it addition, subtraction, multiplication and division can be carried out with great rapidity. Only about a third of time in primary school is left for the rest of the subjects: history, geography, natural science, agricultural knowledge, physical training, singing, drawing and manual labour. Chinese language study is continued for three years in junior high school and then ceases to be taught. The rest of the curriculum for junior and senior high school is very similar to that followed in both USA and UK (secondary) as far as subjects are concerned, with the addition of two periods of politics weekly and some manual work. Geography and history are both very China-centred.

It is estimated that in 1949 there were in China about 200 institutes of higher learning (universities, normal colleges and technical institutes) run by the state, province or missions. Between 1949 and 1952 these were all brought under state control and all mission colleges appropriated. The government's main aim was practical—the training of technicians and cadres. It is claimed that by 1960 just short of 250,000 engineers had been trained. It was not until the 12 Year Science Plan was launched in 1955 that serious attention was turned to the training of pure scientists of doctorate standard. Thereafter great progress in this field was made, as achievements in nuclear power attest, and this in spite of the severe blow dealt to higher education and research when USSR withdrew all its scientists and technicians in 1960. At that time about 65 per cent of university students were training to be teachers and engineers and only about 7 per cent were studying agriculture and forestry. Following the lean years of 1960–1 more students were directed into agriculture and medicine. While university students can express their preferences for particular careers the final determining authority is the State Planning Commission, which has made no secret of its difficulties in co-ordinating supply and demand.

One of China's biggest educational headaches has been the training of an adequate number of teachers. Visiting a big and apparently well-run school near Peking in 1956, the writer was told that the school was woefully understaffed, having only five trained teachers and a number of apprentices (pupil teachers), and for the rest it was lucky if they could read and write. Since then the position has changed greatly for the better but the shortage is still fairly acute. Surprisingly it would seem that differentials in the salaries of the teaching profession are greater than those in industry. There are 12 grades. In universities monthly salaries range from professors at 350 yuan to demonstrators at 60 yuan. In middle and primary schools there are 10 grades, senior teachers receiving 150 yuan per month and kindergarten teachers something between 50 and 25 yuan. The low pay of the lower grades may have some bearing on teacher shortage. Tuition in all grades of school is free as also is lodging. University students are expected to live spartan lives. They receive a small grant to cover simple food costs.

SPARE-TIME EDUCATION AND THE LITERACY CAMPAIGN

Partly because the full-time education programme has been too ambitious of achievement in so short a time, throwing too heavy a burden on the country's economy (in 1960 50 per cent more was being spent on education than on defence), and partly to meet needs outside that programme, a scheme of spare-time education was set in motion in 1955 and has grown to vast proportions. In effect, it is a country-wide programme of adult education, the implementation of which lies largely in the hands of the Trade Unions and communes. It is closely linked with the Literacy Campaign, which has been pursued with vigour ever since Liberation. In those early euphoric days every device was used in this campaign, eg large character posters were stuck up in front of the rickshaw coolie ranks (this sort of transport was soon abolished) and students taught the coolies as they waited for their fares. Night schools were opened everywhere and were attended by old and young. R. F. Price points out in *Education in Communist China* that this literacy drive had its roots away back in World War I when James Y. C. Yen of the YMCA taught the Chinese Labour Corps in France. This led to the establishment of the National Association of Mass Education in 1922, in which Mao Tse-tung was involved. It is estimated that about 90 per cent of the rural population was illiterate in 1949. The percentage was somewhat lower in the towns. By 1960 the percentages were reported as 65 rural and 24 urban and by 1967 it was reckoned that there were few people under the age of 40 who could not read and write.

The achievement of literacy, ie the ability to read 1,500 characters, allows the student (worker) to enter on a course of spare-time education. He or she is guaranteed 240 hours' primary school teaching for two years. This has to be done in addition to ordinary work and is therefore onerous. All the activities such as games, dancing and singing done by the young children in full-time school are dropped and work is concentrated on language and arithmetic. The student can then graduate to a high school course of two years, which is devoted largely to practical, scientific and political subjects. The staffing of these courses is mainly in the hands of skilled workers and full-time teachers doing overtime and receiving extra pay. More often than not the classroom is the factory or workshop.

Successful students can then embark on an arduous university course covering five to six years of evening classes.

In addition to full-time schools and the spare-time system there are also very many part-work part-study schools. These are often associated with a particular industry, such as tea growing and processing and sericulture. Most of the classroom work is done during the slack seasons followed by intensive work in field or factory. In this way students are able to 'pay for their keep' and also have a sense of satisfaction in taking part in real production. Mention must also be made of the significant part played by the PLA in the country's educational system, remembering that 'redness' is more important than 'expertness' in Chinese Communist eyes. The PLA is a great school of cadres. Soldiers emerge from the forces both red and expert, both politically correct and expert in some department of industry or agriculture.

THE GPCR AND EDUCATION

It was this educational set-up which was plunged into turmoil on the outbreak of the GPCR. As we have seen (Chapter 3, p 58) the first shots in the battle between Mao Tse-tung and Liu Shao-ch'i were fired in Peking University in 1966. Liu was charged with fostering the intellectuals, with securing places in schools and universities for them at the expense of the workers and peasants, and, in so doing, with creating rather than destroying class distinctions; in fact, with promoting the very thing against which Mao was constantly on guard, ie the restoration of the intellectuals as an élite class. Mao countered with a reiteration of his faith in the masses and in an educational policy and organisation which enabled everyone, no matter how humble, 'to develop morally, intellectually and physically to become a worker with both socialist consciousness and culture'. While he does not denigrate the intellect, his emphasis is always on the moral (political) and practical. In the turmoil all universities and high schools were closed and all organised education came to a standstill. High schools did not re-open until 1969 and universities until 1971.

Since then the reorganisation of education has been very much on an *ad hoc* and experimental basis. Conditions vary from district to district and are liable to change. As in industry so in schools and colleges, control now lies in the hands of revolutionary committees composed of workers or peasants, teachers and students. Apparently the provincial educational authorities have handed over a good deal of control of time-table and curriculum, which is simplified and more orientated to Mao Tse-tung's thought. University courses have been shortened in most cases from 5 years to 2 or 3, high schools from 6 to 4 and primary from 6 to 5. Great emphasis is placed on education through work. giving effect to Mao's *On Practice*. Part-work part-study is much more the order of the day, students going into the fields or workshop for their maths and science. A compulsory period of two years' practical work between high school and university is now required. Examinations, as understood in the West, have been discarded as divisive and contributing to class consciousness. A good deal of pressure is also being brought to bear on all intellectuals to take a greater part in physical work, thus integrating them more with the masses.

China's educational world at present is still experimenting and 'what's to come is still unsure'.

7

How They Get About

It will be easier for North American readers than British to appreciate the problems of communication which have to be faced in China, if for no other reason than size. Here are a few comparative distances as the crow flies: from Vancouver to Toronto is just about the same mileage as from Shanghai to Kashgar, ie 2,160 miles; New York to San Francisco, 2,680; Canton to Harbin 1,920; Peking to Harbin 650. The longest distance in Great Britain, ie from John o'Groats to Land's End, is only 600 miles.

EARLY COMMUNICATIONS

These long distances posed constant problems for successive Chinese emperors and their success or failure rested very largely on their ability to cope. Their problems were not lessened by the great variety of terrain which had to be traversed. Generally speaking it was the vigorous rulers of new dynasties who tackled the problems and their decadent successors who, by neglecting them, assisted their own downfall. Notable successes were the early Han emperors (206 BC), who maintained the Imperial Silk Route from Sian to Kashgar, and the Mongols (Yuan dynasty 1279–1369), who, by the use of their sturdy ponies and elaborate posting, developed the most efficient communication system over a vast empire ever witnessed before the modern era of rail and internal combustion engine.

Throughout the centuries the way by which the common people got about everywhere in China Proper was by Shanks's pony. Both long and short journeys were normally undertaken on foot. This is still largely true even in these days of developing modern transport—and hard work it can be. If a peasant tells you that it is 6 li from A to B but 4 li from B to A, he is not trying to be funny but is merely expressing distance in terms of effort, it being uphill from A to B.

In the north on the North China Plain and in the loess region high-wheeled, iron-rimmed carts drawn by ponies, oxen or mules where the common means of transport until recently. Outside the towns wide dirt tracks, which served as roads, became badly rutted and very difficult in the summer rains. The carts cut deep into the loess so that a narrow track might be as much as 10–15ft below the surrounding land. Camels were—and still are—used for transport over the desert lands of the north-west.

In central and south China wheeled transport, other than wheelbarrow, was virtually non-existent. All movement of goods was by shrill-squeaking Chinese wheelbarrow or on men's shoulders by carrying pole. 'Roads', seldom more than 6ft wide, might be paved with rough slabs of stone in parts—the work of some public-spirited citizen seeking merit. The unpaved longer sections were deep-rutted by the wheelbarrows in the wet summer. Passengers, other than those travelling on foot, were carried either in *chiao tze* (sedan chairs) or on donkeys. It was common until quite recently to see old folk or sick, wrapped in *pei wo* (cotton bedding quilt), travelling by wheelbarrow.

MODERN ROADS

Little modern road building was undertaken until the 1930s when many hundreds of miles were constructed by the KMT in their attempt to exterminate the CCP, and later during the Sino-Japanese war. The Burma Road was built in 1937–9 to carry supplies over 'The Hump' from Burma to the Chinese army in Szechwan. Few of the highways constructed were all-weather roads; many became impassable in the summer rains. Upkeep was minimal during the civil war between the KMT and CCP (1946–9), with a result that when the Nationalists retreated to Taiwan, road communication was in a shocking state.

For some time after Liberation priority was given to railway development. Nevertheless steady progress was made in road building so that today there are arterial roads to all parts of the country. These are macadamised all-weather roads but have not the surface of American and European motorways. Already there is a fair network of motor roads within densely populated China Proper. From Lanchow to Urumchi (Ti-hua) and to Kashgar (Su-fu) the road runs over long stretches of desert where shifting sands are a constant menace; from Lanchow via Sining and the Tsaidam the road runs over the bleak plateau of Tibet to Lhasa; from Chengtu it cuts across the deep ravines and high longitudinal ridges of Chamdo to Lhasa; from Peking the Gobi desert is crossed to Ulan Baator, the capital of Outer Mongolia, and from Peking two highways link with the developed network of the North-East. Freight carried by motor vehicles in 1958 was small as compared with railways, being only 6,960 million ton-km.

Less spectacular but of great importance are the lateral roads running from the highways in China Proper and forming an ever-increasing web. These are almost entirely the work of the communes, achieved at little capital cost to central or provincial authorities. Along these roads ply country buses, bicycles in their millions, wheelbarrows whose squeaking wheels have been replaced by bicycle wheels with pneumatic tyres, carts whose narrow iron-clad rims have been replaced by motor-car wheels. It is difficult to realise what an enormous economy in effort has been achieved by the introduction of the pneumatic tyre to China.

Slum clearance and the building of new cities have led to the construction of wide roads, lined with trees, in urban areas.

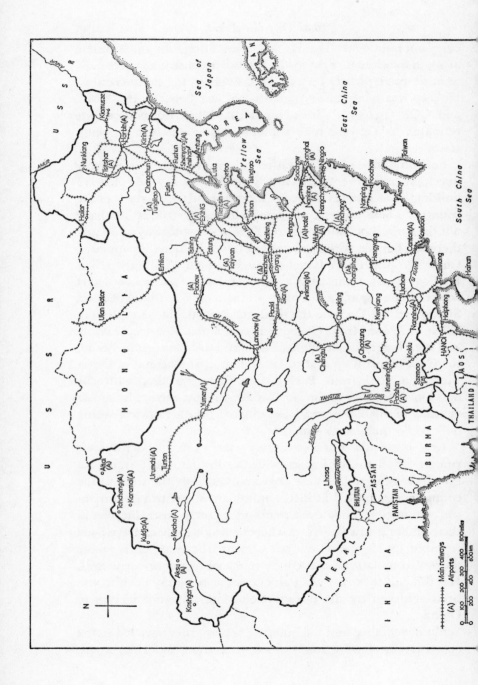

These new roads are remarkable for the scarcity of motors on them although traffic lanes are provided. While the side lanes are crammed with cyclists, public buses and trolley buses enjoy almost exclusive use of the centre lanes. The reason for this is that there are virtually no privately-owned cars. Saloon cars that do ply—and they have increased considerably recently— are for official use and for honoured visitors. Thus, so far, China has not experienced the Western joys of traffic jams at rush hour, the weekend exodus procession and air pollution. It may be that she will yet be spared the motor madness of the Western world.

RAIL

There was a short abortive attempt by foreign enterprise in 1876 to build a railway between Shanghai and Woosung. Official conservatism and local invocation of *feng shui* (the spirit of wind and water) were enough to put a stop to the venture. The rails were torn up and shipped to Japan. Then, in 1886, a short line was built to the Tongshan mines but no real interest was shown until the close of the century, when a spate of railway construction ensued. Foreign companies (British, French, Belgian, German and Dutch) vied with each other to secure concessions. Between 1903 and 1912 ten lines were opened, totalling 5,149 miles, 1,600 of which were in Manchuria where the Russians and Japanese were in competition. The Russian-built Chinese Eastern Railway was 5ft gauge. Japan took over the whole system in the north-east after defeating the Russians in the war of 1904 and reduced it all to standard gauge (4ft 8½in). The most notable lines built during this period were those from Peking to Mukden (Shenyang), 525 miles; from Peking to Hankow, 755 miles; from Tientsin to Pukow, 629 miles. The last two reached the Yangtze, across which trains had to be ferried to connect with the termini of railways built from Wuchang to Changsha and from Nanking to Shanghai respectively. One remarkable railway, which was

I

built by the French during this period, was a narrow-gauge line from Kaiphong to Yunnan. It ran through most difficult country involving the construction of innumerable bridges, culverts and tunnels.

The long troublous period of civil and international strife which followed the formation of the Republic of China (1911) was inimical to railway development. There was a short optimistic period between 1928 and 1937, which led to a minor boom during which some 2,250 miles of track were laid in China Proper, including the extension of the Wuchang–Changsha line to Canton and Kowloon. Japan continued to develop her network throughout this period, having annexed Manchuria and renamed it Manchukuo. The period is remarkable more for the deterioration of lines, bridges and rolling stock than for any new development. Rail travel in the years 1946–9 after long years of neglect during the Sino-Japanese war was precarious. One journeyed in faith. Trains were so overcrowded that many passengers travelled on the roof and were in danger of being swept off at every tunnel. Timber-propped bridges creaked and groaned as the train crawled over them at 2mph. The sight of the bones of a former, less successful train lying in the mud below was not reassuring. In 1949 the nominal mileage for the entire country was 12,036, a large part of which was virtually unusable.

When the People's Government came into power in 1949 it very wisely gave first priority in the field of communications to railway restoration and construction. Some idea of the importance it gave to this development can be gleaned from the proportion of total state investment it earmarked in the first two Five-Year Plans for communications generally and for railways in particular. In the first FYP (1953–8) 17·1 per cent went to communications: railways took 13·3 per cent. In the second FYP (1958–63) the figures were even higher, being 20·9 per cent and 15·5 per cent respectively. The years 1949–52 were devoted almost exclusively to restoration. It is claimed that 3,062 miles of track were restored in that time. Unless actually experienced it is difficult to appreciate the change that was effected in so short a time. The track now permitted speeds of over 40mph instead of a precarious 20mph; bridges no longer filled one with a sense of impending doom; the trains ran pretty well to time and the coaches were clean and not too crowded. This progress has continued with the years. The cleanliness of the streets in the towns, noted earlier, is repeated in the stations, which are spotless. Woe betide the careless one, whose litter will quickly be returned to him, possibly by a child of tender years, with a reminder of civic responsibility.

By the end of the first FYP in 1958 over 6,000 miles of new track had been laid and nearly 1,000 miles of important single line had been double-tracked. By 1960—the last year of published rail statistics—China had about 25,000 miles of track; building was still going ahead but not as rapidly as before. This growth has been the result of a combination of modern techniques and abundant man-power. The planners have had an eye to both economic and strategic requirements. The Lunghai railway has been double-tracked from Suchow to Lanchow, whence it has been extended across the grasslands and deserts via Yumen and Turfan to Urumchi, thus linking the outlying Uighur Autonomous Region of Sinkiang with the central government and also providing transport for the products of the Tarim basin and the oil of Dzungaria. The original intention had been to continue this railway to the Dzungarian Gate to link with the USSR line to Aktogay but building stopped after the rift between the two countries in 1960. The journey from Peking to Urumchi, which formerly could be done only by camel caravan taking months, can now be made in 3–4 days. Other lines of strategic importance are those built to Foochow and Amoy to meet any threat from the KMT in Taiwan and that from Nanning to the North Vietnam border. Peking is now linked by rail across the Gobi desert with Ulan Baator, capital of Outer Mongolia. A railway which has taxed Chinese engineering skill, and one of which they are particularly proud to have brought to a successful conclusion, is the comparatively short line from Chengtu in Szechwan to Paoki on the Wei-ho in Shensi. This cuts through the very difficult highland terrain on the eastern edge of the Tibetan plateau, thus linking the fertile Red Basin with the Hwang-ho. No rail link with Tibet is contemplated at present. These trunk lines were built with capital and expertise provided from central funds. Most of the lateral development (branch lines, feeder lines to mines, forestry narrow-gauge lines) has been done by local labour and local capital from the communes and is cited as a good example of 'walking on two legs'. Great ingenuity and local initiative were shown in the early stages when all kinds of renovated rolling stock and locally made cast iron rails were used.

Railways in China are by far the most important modern means of freight carriage. In 1958 they carried 185,520 million ton-km as compared with motor 6,960 million ton-km and ships and barges 43,910 million ton-km, but these figures are misleading unless the immense but unmeasured amounts of goods borne in native craft on water and pushed or carried on men's shoulders are kept in mind. Although great strides have been made in rail transport, China is still inadequately served in comparison with her needs. Her planners are severely taxed to keep transport facilities and demand in balance and, when sudden unexpected strains are experienced (as in the Great Leap Forward and in the GPCR) serious bottlenecks occur.

WATER

Early Chinese civilisation developed in the lower reaches of the Hwang-ho, which, through its floodings and changes of course, was a menace to men rather than a benefactor so far as transport was concerned. It was not until southward expansion had embraced the rich Yangtze and Si-kiang valleys that the value of water transport was properly appreciated and exploited. Imperial capitals in the north came to rely on the tribute grain from the fertile centre and south, transportation of which was possible only by water. Necessity demanded the building of canals. As early as the fourth century AD, the Suen Fang Canal linking the Hwai-ho with the Hwang-ho and the capital, Loyang, had been built. Later, in T'ang times (AD 618–907) the Old and the New Pien Canals connected Kiangtu on the Yangtze with Kaifeng and Loyang and finally, in the reign of Kublai Khan, the Grand Canal was built, giving water transport from Hangchow to Peking. These canals fell into disrepair and disuse during the last 100 years, particularly in face of the competition of the Peking–Hankow and Teintsin–Pukow railways. Since Liberation the Grand Canal has been renovated and enlarged; 200–500 ton barges can now ply along its length. In addition to the big canals, mention must be made of the dense network of small channels and canals which cover the Yangtze delta, the Hwai plain and the Pearl River delta. These serve both for drainage and irrigation and also as 'roads' along which an immense amount of commerce, retail and wholesale, passes.

Naturally, water communications have been—and still are—of greater importance in wet central and southern China than in the dry north. Movement of both goods and people was cheaper and more comfortable by junk. The mighty Yangtze and its tributaries provided a line of communication east and west, which even today is all important, witness the fact that as yet no continuous railway has been built along its valley in spite of its great economic wealth. It is interesting to note that, until the construction of the Burma Road, it was safer, infinitely more comfortable and even quicker to make the journey from Chungking, Szechwan, to Kunming, Yunnan, down the Yangtze, round the cost by sea to Haiphong and up the Red River, a distance of 2,000 miles, rather than attempt the hazardous overland trip of some 500 miles.

In spite of big seasonal change in water level between summer and winter and in spite of the majestic and difficult gorges between Kweichow and Ichang, the Yangtze is navigable for powered boats up to Chungking, over 1,000 miles inland from Shanghai. In summer, when the river is in spate, ocean-going boats of 15,000 tons can reach Wuhan. The river, which was opened to foreign shipping by the Treaty of Tientsin, 1858, is now closed to all but Chinese bottoms. Some good work was done in the early decades of this century by the provision of navigation lights. Since 1949 a great deal more has been done. Dangerous rocks in the gorges have been blasted, making passage much safer. Four-decker, powerful 'East is Red 37' motor vessels, carrying 1,000 passengers and 200 tons of cargo, are now able to force their way up to Chungking in safety. These have replaced the wretched tracker gangs, who used to earn a precarious living by hauling junks through the rapids at great risk to themselves and the junk crews.

Water conservancy schemes on so many rivers not only have served to control floods, promote irrigation and generate power but have also controlled the regime of the rivers, evening their seasonal flow and thus improving navigability. This has been particularly true of the Hwang-ho.

While the Yangtze, throughout the centuries, has been a great line of communication between east and west, it has in this century been a barrier to modern transport from north to south. The two railways, Peking to Canton and Tientsin to Shanghai, were both forced to ferry their trains across the river at Wuhan and Nanking respectively. These handicaps have been overcome by the building of two great double-decker bridges, each carrying a double-track railway below and a four-lane motorway above. That at Wuhan, completed in 1956, is over one mile long and that at Nanking, opened in September, 1968, is 6,700 metres. A third bridging of the river has been made at Chungking. In view of the geological and flow conditions, the Chinese have reason to be proud of their engineering feat in these and the many other bridges they have built since 1949.

AIR

Aircraft, in the experience of most Chinese before 1946, meant taking cover from Japanese bombs. Between 1946 and 1949 a semi-official private corporation was developed. On the defeat of the Nationalists the planes were flown to Hong Kong and there impounded. Thus the CCP, apart from such military aircraft as it possessed, had to build up its civil air transport from scratch. For the first ten years China had to rely on foreign countries, notably Russia, for her planes but since then has been aiming steadily at becoming self-sufficient in this field. In those early years air travel and transport were restricted to the most urgent needs, to the movement of official personnel and urgently needed materials. Slowly the service has been expanded, so that today this, the most flexible of all means of travel and transport, is available for the private citizen as well as government official to all parts of this vast country except Tibet. There are some fifty airports, a few of which are of international standard. It is significant to note that no less than nine airports are in Sinkiang.

8

How They Amuse Themselves

THE reader is reminded once again that no part of life in China today can be regarded as apolitical. Every activity is meant to serve the proletarian revolution and this becomes crystal clear when we turn to the cultural side of life. In 1942, well before Liberation, Mao Tse-tung in his *Talks at the Yenan Forum on Education and Art* said:

> *In the world today all culture, all literature and art belong to definite classes and are geared to political lines . . . All our literature and art are for the masses of the people and in the first place for the workers, peasants and soldiers; they are created for the workers, peasants and soldiers and are for their use.*

The old literary and artistic forms, which were the preserve of the gentry in times past, are being remodelled and infused with new content in the service of the people. There is a repudiation of 'art for art's sake' and 'pure music' etc as being bourgeois. Absolute individual freedom in these fields, it is claimed, is only possible when the classless society has been achieved.

The Chinese have a reputation for taking their recreation and amusements quietly. This statement may sound strange when one remembers their love of *reh lao* (hot noise), of the ear-splitting music of their traditional opera, and of their thunderous use of crackers on joyous occasions such as New Year and weddings; it is none the less true. One mark of a gentleman in old China was that he never moved faster than a sedate walk—a fact that militated strongly against the introduction of Western games into schools and colleges in the early part of this century. Typical of amusement at this time was the sight of men, old and young, bird cage in hand in the quiet of the evening, seeking a good tree on which to hang it and near which to sit and listen to the bird's song.

FESTIVALS

Recreation and leisure, however, were largely a luxury of the gentry, who alone could afford to have feasts, throw parties and employ musicians to entertain them. The peasantry relied very largely on festivals for their excitement and, for many of them, their taste of meat. By far the most important of these festivals was—and still is—Chinese New Year, which fell at the end of January. Since 1949 its date has been changed to 1 January (international calendar) to comply with world usage. This is the time for family reunions and in pre-Liberation days festivities might be extended for more than a fortnight. The present government has tried to shorten this time but, according to reports, with only limited success. Homes are spring-cleaned, special provisions including *po po* (white flour dumplings) eaten by high and low alike, the kitchen god propitiated (his place is now mainly taken by a photo of Mao Tse-tung), congratulatory sentences (formerly door-gods) pasted on the front door panels and crackers galore let off. The succeeding days are spent on jollification and in visiting relations and friends. Formerly there were special days on which men went visiting (1st to 8th and women sallied forth (8th to 15th). The 10th to 30th of the Chinese calendar were considered good days for weddings. How far such ideas still obtain it is difficult to estimate in face of Communist propaganda against all superstition. It is probable that people in remote rural districts still cling to many of the old ideas. New Year is a season during which, like Christmastide in the West, a spirit of good will to all men pervades the air.

Another festival, which in earlier times was of great importance and was strictly observed, was *Ch'ing Ming* (Pure Brightness), when families visited their ancestral graves carrying sprays of willow or blossom, together with sacrificial utensils, paper money and paper models of such things as they thought their forebears needed. The sacrifices were made, the money and models burned and the grave mounds swept and tidied. The family then gathered to have a picnic meal in company with the spirits of their ancestors. While this custom is not stressed under the present regime, it is still widely observed and enjoyed. In Peking today *Ch'ing Ming* is made the occasion for 'round the houses' races in which thousands of men and women take part.

On the fifth day of the fifth month (Chinese calendar) the Dragon Boat or 'Upright Sun' Festival is held, when teams of as many as forty rowers in long canoes race with each other. Every town and village of any considerable size in central and south China sited by river or lake boasts of at least one 'dragon boat'. These races are very popular and create great excitement and rivalry. Ssu Ma-ch'ien, China's great historian (145–86 BC), records how Ch'u Yuan, a famous poet, disgusted with the political state of his time, committed suicide in the Mo Li river, near Changsha, by clasping a stone and throwing himself into the water. Tradition has it that people put out in boats to recover his body and every year thereafter threw rice over the water for him from their boats. It may be that this was the origin of the custom. It is more likely, however, that this is an old fertility rite. The fifth month is the time when rains are wanted for the rice and the dragon boat races are an attempt to induce the dragons of the air to disgorge their moisture. The fact that this festival is more popular in the rice-growing than in the wheat-growing lands lends credence to this explanation.

The date of the festival commemorating the formation of the Republic in 1911 is fixed variously by the two claimants to be the true representatives of China, namely, CCP and KMT. The former hold their national celebrations on the 1st of the 10th month and the latter hold theirs on the 10th of the 10th month. This difference matters little so long as the KMT celebrate in isolation in Taiwan but it does present the Hong

Kong government with grave tensions when the jollifications of the two opposing sides take place in such close proximity.

These national celebrations on Mainland China take the form of huge parades in which all sections of the people take part. These parades occur in all large cities but, naturally, the most spectacular is seen in Peking, when many hundreds of thousands assemble in the People's Square to march past and salute Mao Tse-tung and his ministers as they stand on the terrace of *T'ien An Men* (the Gate of Heavenly Peace) on May Day. These parades are significant in many ways. The standing of ministers is demonstrated by their juxtaposition to Chairman Mao. They satisfy the desire for the grand spectacle, particularly as the masses fully participate, something quite lacking from their experience in the past. The parades also reflect a high capacity for organisation and orderliness; it is no mean job to put on a march past of hundreds of thousands of workers, peasants, minorities, soldiers and school children marching in dressed ranks 20–30 abreast, with banners flying. The Square in which these massive assemblies take place is, itself, impressive if only for its size. It lies south of T'ien An Men and is flanked on the west by the People's Assembly Hall, the Chinese equivalent of the Capitol. Its great hall will seat 10,000 people and its banqueting hall 5,000. On the east lies the Museum of History and the Revolution and on the south the Memorial to the People's Heroes, a tall monolith round the base of which are a Mao Tse-tung quotation and bas-relief carvings of historical events from the Opium War onward. Festivals today have lost much of their significance as holidays because the working week is now 5½ days. Sunday (*Hsin Ch'i Ih*) is a rest day, when family visits to the parks and museums and boating on the lake are the order of the day.

OLD AMUSEMENTS

In former times itinerant players visited temples and villages on fair days and feast days bringing with them their performing bears, dogs, monkeys, mice and their puppets. Plays enacting old legends and well-known fairy tales were put on; acrobats, jugglers and stilt-walkers were there and, above all, the professional story-teller, always popular in town and country alike. Today these actors and entertainers have, very largely, been incorporated into official professional troupes whose job is both to entertain and 'to spread the gospel of socialism and Mao Tse-tung's thought'. As in the West, their skill and artistry in acrobatics, balancing, juggling and tightrope walking, always of a high order, has been developed to an incredible degree. The troupes travel widely to the steppelands of Inner Mongolia, to Sinkiang and the wilds of Tibet and the Autonomous Minorities. The story-teller is still in great demand but his stories are now of the heroes and heroines of the revolution and of the tyrannies of feudal landlord oppression.

There was not a great variety of games played by adults. There were many card games, played with Chinese playing cards, and there was also mahjong. All of these involved gambling. The one honourable exception was chess, which some Chinese claim as originating in their own country rather than Persia. They have two varieties of chess, *hsiang ch'i* and *wei ch'i*. The former is similar to international chess; the strategy is very much the same and the movement of some of the pieces is almost identical, although they have, of course, different names. *Wei ch'i* is the Chinese variation of the Japanese game *go*.

The children had—and still have—many simple games, which vary with the seasons. They are particularly skilful at a game usually played in a circle. It involves passing a shuttlecock from one to another by kicking it with the side of the heel. It is also played individually with great skill. In earlier days the shuttlecock was made by binding together two or three 'cash' (the old copper coin with a hole through the middle) and attaching a few feathers. This and hopscotch were popular during the winter months. Their place was taken by kite flying in the warmer days. Kites of all shapes and sizes with elaborate tails are made. They are flown individually, or in competition with the strings covered with powdered glass and glue, the object being to saw across your opponent's string and cut his kite free. These games are still played but they are being superseded to a large degree by Western games, notably ping-pong, which is played in earnest in primary school.

SPORT

Although the gentleman and the scholar restricted his movements to a slow, dignified walk, he could and did engage in *t'ai chi ch'uan*, (*t'ai chi*, the ultimate principle of Chinese philosophy; *ch'uan*, fist or boxing). This is a form of physical exercise which involves slow, smooth rhythmic movements and demands a high degree of muscular control. Like yoga, it has a philosophical basis, being related to Taoism. It is practised mainly by the old and middle-aged but it is not despised by the young. Its devotees can be seen in the parks and any open space every morning doing their exercises. *T'ai chi ch'uan*, which is essentially an individual activity, was extended long ago to exercises between two people, often using swords and spears. This 'boxing' involved rapid and violent aggressive movements, the boxers never touching each other. It was early incorporated into Chinese opera. Skating was indulged in in the north, the emperor making a special award for skill each year. Today it is a popular sport.

The move from the old attitude towards physical exertion to the Western outlook on sports and team games was revolutionary and did not take place without opposition. Students in mission schools held to the traditional standards of scholastic behaviour. They wore long gowns and walked sedately. However, when the change did come in the early decades of the twentieth century, it came quickly and team games and athletics were taken up with alacrity. It is interesting to remember that one of Mao Tse-tung's earliest enthusiasms was physical fitness; his first publications were concerned with physical culture. Today, one of his much-quoted slogans is 'Promote physical culture and build up health.' Once Western games had been accepted, students embraced them whole-heartedly and quickly developed a high degree of skill, particularly in soccer, basket ball, athletics and gymnastics. Even as early as 1924, Wesley College, at which the writer taught, had a soccer team, which could play and beat most of the British gunboat teams that came up to Hankow. It also had a hockey team, which could give the Hankow Race Club a good game.

Since those days Chinese prowess in all departments of sport has achieved international standards. It is reported that Ni Chih-chin cleared 2·29 metres in the high jump on 8 November 1971. Now that Mainland China is a member of UN and barriers to intercourse are breaking down, it is to be hoped that her sports and athletic teams will soon be competing at the Olympic Games. The game, however, in which China has already entered into full international competition and in which she has shown great skill is ping-pong. It is played everywhere, indoors and out-of-doors in the dry season and at all levels from primary school upwards. China has used the game skilfully to further and foster friendly international relations. Another field in which the Chinese have shown aptitude and enthusiasm is swimming. Maybe this is due, in part, to the example set by Mao Tse-tung, who in his younger days used to swim the Yangtze at Wuhan where the river is a mile wide and in summer when it is in full spate—no mean achievement. Every large city today has its sports stadium, its swimming pool and its children's palace for the furtherance of physical fitness.

THEATRE

Wherever one goes in China Proper it is unusual not to find somewhere within the precincts of any town a stage, often of bamboo in the south, facing an open space available for travelling troupes of players. Larger towns and cities have their playhouses and theatres or opera houses, the most famous being in

Peking and Canton. In these, until the fall of the Manchu dynasty in 1911, plays and operas of the old classical tradition were presented, depicting scenes of comedy and tragedy from feudal life in old China, of court intrigue and the clever stratagems in history all intermixed with spirits and demons. There was no tradition of high dramatic art such as characterised Shakespearian England. The theatre's idiom was a mixture of singing, talking, dancing, clowning, tumbling and acrobatics. Presentation was highly stylised and stereotyped: the character of the actor (hero, villain, general, clown etc) was indicated by the make-up or mask worn; the props he carried indicated the situation in which he found himself, eg a tasselled whip and he was mounted, or an oar and he was in a boat; the scenery was conventional and simply representative, eg a lantern indicated night, an embroidered curtain a bed. The theatre itself was reminiscent of Shakespeare's England in that the stage stood right out into the auditorium with the audience on three sides. However, the groundlings, who in Elizabethan days stood in the pit round the stage, were relegated in China to the back seats, while the élite enjoyed seats, tables and tea near the stage. The orchestra (strings, clappers, cymbals, trumpets and flutes) sat in full view on the stage and formed an integral and important part of the proceedings. The crescendo of noise as some crisis of action approached was deafening.

It was not until World War I that Western drama made any impact on China. At that time a literary movement, led by Hu Shih and Soong Tsung-fang, was afoot, calling for a discarding of the old feudal shapes and ideas. Students returning from abroad started the Spring Willow Dramatic Society in Peking in 1915. At first rather poor grade plays were put on but quite soon Shakespeare, Ibsen, Chekhov and Shaw were being presented to audiences in big new Western theatres in Peking and Shanghai. The Western theatre was used to foster national resistance to Japanese aggression between 1931 and 1937. Western drama, popular among the sophisticated in the cities, was not understood by and made no impact on the masses. It should be recorded that the Chinese as a whole have consider-

able natural histrionic gifts, especially in mimicry and im-
promptu prodcution.

During the Yenan period (1935–49) the Communists became
acquainted with Shensi folk songs and in particular with a
harvest dance, the Yanko, which they adopted and used in
subsequent years to great effect in promoting a sense of unity
and camaraderie. While the dance has many refinements, it is
basically simple, having just three forward steps and one backward and sideways. In the early years of Liberation it became
the national dance. On a shopping expedition one would meet
a line of dancers coming up the street and would join in for a
hundred yards or so and then break off. From these beginnings
the new regime has transformed the Chinese theatre and opera.
The old feudal and imperial themes with their princes, courtiers
and concubines have been discarded and replaced by stories of
heroic deeds by peasants and workers against the Japanese in-
vader or tales of oppression suffered by the masses at the hands
of landlords.

The new idiom borrows from both the Chinese classical and
the Western theatre, using the symbolism of the former and the
realism of the latter. Outstanding early plays, which are still
running, are *The White-Haired Girl* and *Chou Tsi-shan*. All
modern revolutionary Peking operas have clear political teaching and are intended to stimulate revolutionary fervour. *Taking
Tiger Mountain by Strategy*, *The Red Lantern*, *The East is Red* and
Shachiapang depict the PLA and the Chinese people in their
life-and-death struggles with the Japanese and have their full
quota of heroes, heroines, traitors, imperialist enemies and
wicked landlords. In the latest opera *On the Docks* the scene is
shifted to the waterfront where the heroine, Fang Hai-chen,
leads the class struggle against traitorous counter-revolutionary
sabotage. The ballet *The Red Detachment of Women*, first produced in 1964, is claimed to be *the* break with the past in this
field because its theme is of workers, peasants and soldiers instead of 'kings, nobles, fairies and phantoms'. Mao, comment-
ing on it in 1964, said, 'The orientation is correct, the revolution-
isation successful and the artistic quality good.' Although

actors are named on programmes, stardom in the theatre world is avoided as far as possible. Parts are often doubled so that only the knowledgeable in the audience will be aware which of the two is on the stage at the moment.

Theatre going is now part of everyday life of the masses. It forms an important part of communication. Tickets are cheap and are apportioned to factories, schools etc and the actors play to packed audiences. Amateur dramatic societies are very popular and many are of high standard.

CINEMA

Films, like the theatre, have been harnessed to the service of the revolution. Those which are of Chinese production deal, almost entirely, with anti-feudal and anti-imperialist themes. Foreign films are mainly Russian. For example, two films *Lenin in October* and *Lenin in 1918* were shown throughout the country on the occasion of the 100th anniversary of his birth and were very popular. Children's films are mainly cartoons and are politically (ie morally) educative, teaching unselfishness and service of the people. Typical is *Heroic Sisters on the Grasslands*, a true story of two young girls on Inner Mongolian grasslands, telling of their progress and heroic deeds as they are brought up on Mao Tse-tung's Thought.

LITERATURE

Early Chinese fiction has become known to the West largely through translations, such as Arthur Walley's *Monkey*, which comes from *Pilgrimage to the West*, and Pearl Buck's *All Men are Brothers*, which tells in English the *Stories of the Fringes of the Marsh*. These, together with the ever-popular *Dream of the Red Chamber* (about 1765) and many others of this period, are stories in Robin Hood vein of the righteous outlaw fighting against the established oppressors. They are, consequently, in

K

full favour today and are widely read but were banned under the Manchu dynasty. In the early 1920s there was a revival of fiction writing led by Hu Shih, Lu Hsun and Kuo Mo-jo. Lu Hsun's best-known novel is *The True Story of Ah Q*.

Since Liberation there has been a tremendous output of writing, which, in the present political climate, must conform to the requirements laid down by Mao in his *Talks at the Yenen Forum on Art and Literature*, ie it must be written for and have as its objective the service of the people. This sounds—and is—restrictive but, since this objective is open to interpretation, it has the virtue of creating endless debate. Writing on this point Edgar Snow says, 'Non-conformist art is an introspective luxury which only affluent and stable societies can afford'. The development of the wall newspaper has inspired all and sundry in commune, factory, army and school to try their hands at writing and, most notably, at poetry, giving the authors a sense of participation and some satisfaction of the creative urge.

In addition to the *Jen-min Jih-pao*, the *People's Daily*, which is the newspaper reflecting the official voice from Peking, there are other national newspapers, such as the *Ta Kung Pao*. Every province has its own daily and many cities besides. Hundreds of magazines and journals serve the societies and special interests throughout the land.

ART

Chinese art is, at present, undergoing as great an upheaval as that experienced by Western art during the last century. While the West has been busy repudiating realism and turning to symbolism, China, in the judgement of some experts, is turning in the opposite direction from her traditional landscape concepts in which, if man figures at all, he falls unobtrusively into the scene as a whole, to Socialist Realist presentation in which the dominant figure is muscular, truculent man. Michael Sullivan, writing in 1959 in his *Chinese Art in the Twentieth Century* says, 'The majority of Chinese painters have rejected the way of life and the attitude to the world which constituted the symbolic content of their art. They are now absorbed in the world of reality.' Here again, the artist, like the rest, is required to make his art 'serve the people'. A few acknowledged masters, such as Ch'i Pai-shih (1861–1957), have been able to carry on working in the old tradition but the vast majority of traditionalists have had to bow to the political wind. Continuing to paint in the old idiom, some have attempted to satisfy ideological demands by incorporating a quotation from Mao Tse-tung's writings. Others have tried to combine the two schools, generally with disastrous results. Each school has its own distinct philosophy, each has its own methods of depicting perspective and any attempt to mix them seems doomed to failure. During and since the GPCR the objective of serving the masses has been more strictly required of the artist. As with literature, so with art, there has been a great upsurge of effort and output; anyone can try his hand in a field of expression denied to many in the past.

Sculpture has never figured prominently in China, save for Buddhist influence. Today clay modelling is popular, vigorous and realistic. It has been used lavishly in the revolutionary drive, eg *Rent Collection Courtyard*, an exhibition in six scenes of life-sized clay figures vividly portraying landlord oppression of the peasantry. Applied art in many fields, particularly ceramics, flourishes.

MUSIC

The great revolution which has swept China has dealt more kindly with music than with art. The music of the old opera, played by *hu ch'in* (Chinese fiddle), flute, harp and *p'i pa* (a kind of zither), was challenged by the same group as introduced Western drama in the 1920s. Western music has received much easier and more widespread acceptance than has Western drama. The Shanghai Conservatory, founded in the 1920s, is today China's leading music academy. The Chinese have shown remarkable aptitude in mastering Western instruments particularly piano, strings and woodwind. Symphony orchestras, playing Western classical music, were formed in the 1930s; their number has been greatly increased since Liberation. They have developed their own musical idiom, a blend of their own tradition and Western classical with a distinct Russian flavour. The same ideological outlook is demanded of music as is required of the other arts. The latest big production is the *Yellow River Concerto*, an adaptation of the *Yellow River Cantata*, composed by Hsien Hsing-hai in Yenan in 1939. It has four movements: Yellow River Boatmen; Ode to the Yellow River; The Yellow River Roars; Defeat of the Yellow River. This concerto, it is claimed, is the answer to 'subjective, bourgeois, idealist musicians'.

RADIO AND TELEVISION

Radio is, perhaps, the chief medium of communication between government and people. Loudspeakers are ubiquitous and incessant. Transistors are now available at reasonable prices to the masses. Those who have travelled in China will appreciate that one of the luxuries of first class rail travel is the privilege of being able to switch off the radio. Television is available, at present, only on local circuit but a nationwide service is predicted in the near future.

MUSEUMS AND ART GALLERIES

Until the GPCR in 1966, visiting museums, art galleries and exhibitions was a popular recreation of great numbers of people. This was brought to an abrupt end when the Red Guards in misdirected zeal attacked anything savouring of the past. All museums and galleries were hastily closed and, only now in 1972, are being slowly re-opened. Exhibitions, such as that of the *Staircase Scheme* for control of the Hwang-ho, showing projected plans or actual achievements in production, water conservancy, communications etc, have been a popular way of maintaining public interest and involvement.

9

Hints to Visitors

VISITORS will be well aware that they are entering a country that has a great and distinguished past—the only ancient civilisation which has continued uninterrupted to the present day. In spite of the fact that the Chinese are today embracing with enthusiasm an entirely new philsophy and way of life, they are, none the less, proud of their heritage and of its past achievements. Since the tourist is likely to be in the country for a mere three to four weeks, he will get the greatest value from his stay only if a fair amount of reading is done in preparation.

ENTRY

Permission to enter can be obtained by single individuals simply by application to the Chinese Embassy but, more usually, permission is granted to groups, whether they be business men, athletes or simply sight-seeing tourists. Only highly privileged visitors are permitted to travel freely beyond the five or six prescribed tours, which include the main cities of Peking, Sian, Shanghai, Wuhan, Hangchow and Canton, where factories, schools, hospitals, theatres and communes will be visited. Trips to famous historical sites, such as the Great Wall and the Ming Tombs, are included.

Since very few visitors to China are able to speak the language, interpreters are essential. Experience has proved them to be friendly and invaluable guides. When the trip for the day is over, the visitor is free to wander the streets at will. Television programmes in the West have made it generally known that the greeting, when one is introduced to a group, is hand-clapping. The correct and polite response is to clap in return.

WHEN

Westerners generally find that the weather in China in September and October suits them best. The summer rains are over, the skies are clear and the temperature is not too warm. Mid-winter in the north is bitterly cold, days are short and dust storms fairly frequent. Mid-summer (June, July and August) everywhere is very hot and in central and southern China the relative humidity is high and very enervating.

PERSONAL

A fair supply of clothes to meet the seasonal claims should be taken. All normal personal requirements are readily available at the stores. Plenty of colour film should be taken as Chinese colour film has to be processed locally. It is advisable to take plenty of English reading material as little is available in the bookshops. Few, if any, foreign newspapers can be had.

HOTELS

Foreign visitors are housed in modern hotels, which are very comfortable and have all modern services, including laundry. Both Chinese and good Western food is served.

MONEY

Since payment for all expenses (travel, hotel, etc) is made before entry, the only money the visitor requires is for incidental expenditure. There is no tipping. Wages in China are low but the purchasing power of the yuan is high, ie in terms of £ and $ things are cheap.

ANTIQUES AND WORKS OF ART

If any of these are bought, it is essential to obtain a stamped permission from the dealer. If this is done, no difficulty is then experienced in customs on exit.

Bibliography

Adams, Ruth (ed). *Contemporary China* (1969)

Buchanan, K. *The Chinese People and the Chinese Earth* (1966)

Chen, H. E. (ed). *The Chinese Communist Regime, Documents and Commentary* (1967)

Chen, Jack. *The Chinese Theatre* (1949)

Chen, Jerome. *Mao and the Chinese Revolution* (1965)

Dawson, R. (ed). *The Legacy of China* (1964)

Donnithorne, A. *China's Economic System* (1967)

Eberhard, W. *A History of China* (1948)

Fitzgerald, C. P. *Flood Tide in China* (1958)

——. *The Chinese View of Their Place in the World* (1965)

Greene, Felix. *The Wall Has Two Sides* (1963)

Han Suyin. *China in the Year 2001* (1967)

Lu Hsun. *A Brief History of Chinese Fiction*

MacNair, H. F. (ed). *China* (1946)

Mao Tse-tung. *Selected Works*, 4 vols (1962)

——. *Quotations from Chairman Mao Tse-tung* (The Little Red Book)

Price, R. F. *Education in Communist China* (1970)

Purcell, Victor. *China* (1962)

——. *Problems of Chinese Education* (1936)

Sewell, W. G. *I Stayed in China* (1932)

Snow, Edgar. *The Other Side of the River* (1959)

——. *Red Star over China* (1938)

Tawney, R. H. *Land and Labour in China* (1932)

Tregear, T. R. *A Geography of China* (1965)

——. *Economic Geography of China* (1970)

Wheelwright, E. L. and Macfarlane, B. *The Chinese Road to Socialism* (1970)

Paperbacks
Cottrell, L. *The Tiger of Ch'in* (1964)
Han Suyin. *The Crippled Tree* (1968)
Kuo Ping-chia. *China* (1960)
Schram, S. *Mao Tse-tung* (1966)
Schurmann, F. and Schell, O. *China Readings*, 3 vols (1967)
Snow, Edgar. *Red China Today* (1970)

Acknowledgements

My thanks are due to William Sewell and Maude Poole for the helpful suggestions they have made in reading my manuscript. They are, of course, in no way responsible for its shortcomings.

T. R. T.

Index